Powerful
Persuasion

Powerful Persuasion

Multimedia Witness in Christian Worship

Tex Sample

ABINGDON PRESS
NASHVILLE

POWERFUL PERSUASION
MULTIMEDIA WITNESS IN CHRISTIAN WORSHIP

This book is printed on acid-free paper.

Library of Congress Cataloging-in-Publication Data

Sample, Tex.
    Powerful persuasion : multimedia witness in Christian worship / Tex Sample.
        p. cm.
    Inclues bibliographical references and index.
    ISBN 0-687-33901-4 (binding: adhesive, pbk. : alk. paper)
    1. Public worship—Audio-visual aids. I. Title.

    BV288.S26 2005
    261.5'2—dc22

                                                                2004029018

05 06 07 08 09 10 11 12 13 14—10 9 8 7 6 5 4 3 2 1

MANUFACTURED IN THE UNITED STATES OF AMERICA

For

Theresa Abshagen

Robert E. Bergmark

Paul K. Deats, Jr.

Walter G. Muelder

Contents

Acknowledgments

To have friends is a delight and a "burden." I have always had better friends than I deserve. It is a delight to live in the warmth and the devotion good friends offer. To know this kind of friendship is to be blessed indeed. It is also a burden because I can never repay the kindness of friends, especially those who helped so generously in this effort. So many people read the manuscript, and their comments make it so much better than it would otherwise be. The following read all or part of it: Gene Barnes, Calvin Brister, Eric Elnes, Gilbert Ferrell, Joel Ferrell, Larry Hollon, Gene Lowry, Sarah Lowry, Jeff Procter-Murphy, Dorothy Saunders-Perez, Karen Sue Spencer-Barnes, Bascom Talley, and Laurence Wagley. They cannot be held responsible for what is finally here, but they saved me from many errors and false moves. I appreciate all of them more than I can ever express in words. I just give thanks to God for them.

I dedicate this book to four of my teachers: Theresa Abshagen, Robert Bergmark, Paul Deats, Jr., and Walter Muelder. Ms. Abshagen taught us English in high school; she read us poetry in ways that even the most testosterone-poisoned boy in school could not dismiss. She, moreover, *was* the drama department and formed my love for theater. Professor Bergmark first introduced me to philosophy and to social Christianity. He changed the direction of my life. I first read Marx, Durkheim, and Weber with Professor Deats. I cannot measure the impact of his welcomed influence and personality on my work. Walter Muelder was *the* dean to all of us who studied with him. We often asked him questions just to watch him go to work on an issue. To witness his intellectual power and his capacity to move among diverse theoretical sources remains the most powerful intellectual performance in my experience.

Acknowledgments

My best friend in the world is Peggy Sample. I often say to her that she and Jesus are the best things that ever happened to me. By this I do not mean to diminish the ultimacy of Jesus as Christ or to apotheosize Peggy. Rather, I want to suggest how central her friendship is in my life. It is not only her art, her singing voice, her wide acquaintance with popular culture, but her enormous sensitivity and care for others, the clarity of her love, and the hospitality of her spirit. I have never understood why she married me, but I am so very glad she did.

Introduction

R hetoric is the art of persuasion. It has a rich history. There is also a good deal of conflict about its appropriate use and, often, about whether it can be used at all without being manipulative. This is especially so in the church. How are the practices of persuasion to be used faithfully?

This question is even more contentious today with the rise of electronic and digital culture and the ways in which media are used in powerfully persuasive ways. Can the church use media in worship and witness? If so, how? Is the church simply to become a place of entertainment? Is the church to give itself over to marketing techniques and provide what today's spiritual consumers seek? Are we merely to ask what people want and then attempt to give it to them? After all, some seem to say, "the customer is always right."

Furthermore, the multisensory and multimedia character of so many events today is characterized by an environmental use of image, music, beat, light, movement, and dance. By environmental in this context I mean a spectacle-like, multisensory, multimedia event in which the audience becomes the "performer" in an immersive "capsule of reality." These environmental settings take on a central role in entertainment, sport venues, political rallies, and other settings. They can be profoundly persuasive. In fact, these kinds of events may be the most powerful bonding practices in our culture. They may be the basic forms that practices of commitment take. It is my contention that the most powerful forms of persuasion in the culture are these multisensory and multimedia events. These events are the new form of rhetoric in our culture.

Rhetoric is conditioned by history and culture. It changes over time, and what is persuasive in one time may be an actual "turnoff" in another. I contend that the practices of rhetoric are shifting radically in our time. The persuasive practices of the world of my youth and young adulthood are not those of today. Rather, the practices of rhetoric in the emergent electronic and digital culture are those of "ecological" events in which a synthesis of image, sound, beat, light, movement, and dance engage an audience as performer in the event.

If this be so, what is a faithful response to these practices of rhetoric by the church? I believe media can be used by the church and can play a faithful role in the life and work of the church. This book attempts to lay out ways in which media can be used in ways intrinsic to the faith of the church. This places a new challenge before the church. In its proclamation and witness how does the church articulate the gospel in persuasive forms, but without selling out the faith itself?

This is the focus of this book: How can the church use multisensory and multimedia rhetoric in ways that are intrinsic to, or compatible with, the faith? My response to this question makes up the three parts of the text. The first part seeks to be clear about who we are and whose we are in the church as we attempt to engage contemporary practices. I begin chapter 1 by emphasizing the centrality of God's story and the importance of the church getting its story right. This chapter also addresses the role that faithful practices play in forming us in this story. In chapter 2 I move to the question of how the church negotiates its relationship to the cultures around it. I argue here for the church to "pitch tent" with these cultures in such a way that it joins some practices but opposes others.

In part 2 I turn to the art of rhetoric. Chapter 3 begins with a brief look at rhetoric as the art of persuasion and the ways it can be used for manipulation or for building up the Body of Christ. The chapter then turns to the new form of multisensory and multimedia rhetoric in electronic culture, especially in the integrative synthesis of sensory experience. Chapters 4 through 7 examine the uses of image, music, beat, light, movement, and dance respectively in order to see how each of these functions in new forms of rhetoric. I make here the point that we are not addressing images in the visual sense only but auditory, rhythmic, illuminative, and kinesthetic experience as well for which I use the word *figure*. Chapter 8 brings these multisensory figures together to discuss their holistic impact. That is, the integrative synthesis of image, music, beat, light, move, and dance is greater than the sum of their parts. This impact is considered not only in the ways that each of these figures influences the others but also their holistic role in performance, in story, and in the practice of immersion.

The third part of the book advances the role of multisensory and multimedia rhetoric in the prophetic ministry of the church. It begins in chapter 9 with an exploration of the way that the Hebrew prophets used figures across time to clarify and to expand the relationship of God to the people of Israel. This Hebrew poetry has rich implications for an electronic culture. I discuss these implications in chapter 10 in terms of the role of figure in contemporary culture and the ways that these can be placed in God's story. Chapter 11 concludes this section with the description of what I believe to be a new form of criticism that is different from the critical distance of a print culture. I call this practice *critical immersion.* I demonstrate this practice in multisensory and multimedia events and in worship. I conclude in the epilogue with a summary of the book and with my attempt to provide a concrete illustration of moving toward multisensory and multimedia rhetoric in terms of a vision for my local church.

Two further comments. First, I am sharply aware of the ways that electronic culture is influenced by consumerist capitalism. I am also clear that I want the church to be an alternative to this kind of culture. The uncritical ways that many churches use market models subvert the faith in subtle and not so subtle ways. The free gift of God's grace is not a commodity, and the church is not in the business of selling. For this reason I am quite critical of consumerism throughout the text, and I am at no little pain to distance the work of the church from it.

Second, I am deeply troubled by the supreme power of the United States in the world today. I was raised on Lord Acton's epigram, "power corrupts and absolute power corrupts absolutely." This nation state now holds that kind of corruptive power. There is no country in the world today with power commensurate to check that of the United States. It is a dangerous time. Such power also influences the church. I am concerned about how little prophetic passion comes from the churches, especially in bearing witness that is critical of the nation state. While it is important for the church to be an alternative community in any society, this is an especially important time to do so in our context.

Hence a faithful use of rhetoric, important in any time, takes on new practices in our day. At its heart the witness to the Christian faith is one of persuasion, not of proof, and certainly not of coercion. Furthermore, the faithful use of rhetoric by the church will avoid manipulation. And, finally, if the church is to be an alternative community to that of consumerism and idolatrous nationalism, it will require practices capable of a telling critique of these orders, on the one hand, and persuasive practices intrinsic to the faith that form us in the image of Christ, on the other. In order to find our way here the first step is to get our story right. We begin this in chapter 1.

Part One

Practicing the
Story and
Pitching Tent

Story and Practice

S tanley Hauerwas tells a story about his six-year-old cousin. The little boy is in Sunday school in a church outside Dallas, and his teacher is telling the class about the Crucifixion. While he knows the story of Jesus on the cross, this is the first time in his young life that he begins to understand that the cross is an event of great agony for Jesus. It, of course, disturbs him so he attempts to get the teacher's attention by raising his hand. She fails to notice him, so he begins to wave his hand. When this doesn't work, he stands at his seat and now waves vigorously. Finally getting her attention, he shouts out: "If Roy Rogers had been there the s.o.b.s couldn't have done it!"

Now, I like Roy Rogers. In fact, when I compare his movies to the levels of violence on TV and in the cinema today, it is pretty mild. In those days Roy shoots the gun out of the outlaw's hand. Today's action heroes may first knock their sinister opponents into a giant gear box to be ground into hamburger before being then deposited into a dissolving acid as the last act before placing their "remains" in a rocket ship headed for the surface of the fiery furnace of the sun. Roy is better.

Still, the six-year-old makes the mistake we Christians repeatedly make. We take God's story and we are forever placing it in another story. He and we take the story of a nonviolent savior who has at his disposal, according to scripture, a legion of angels should he want them, but asks for no such violent rescue. He faces the torture, the agony, and death on the cross peaceably. He does not take up the sword.

Getting the Story Right

When I first began to attend church regularly, my Sunday school teacher was a man I shall call Mr. Archon, the New Testament Greek word for *ruler.* It is not his real name. He was quite prominent in my town, a man of some means. What is more he was a charismatic man, a person with a lot of magnetism about him. I don't recall that he ever told anyone what to do. When he wanted something done, he always asked. He never ordered people around. He had a kind of authority about him that made you want to do it. A good teacher in Sunday school, he held our interest, and he convinced us without seeming to demand it.

About once a month it seemed, maybe more often, he taught us that African Americans were not fully human. They were cursed by God, and they were to be ruled over by whites. Segregation of the races was to be maintained at all cost, and it was our responsibility as Southerners, as Mississippians, and as Christians to support the separation of the races and the rule of whites.

It just so happens that there was a retired missionary, Miss Harriet Annette Buehl (not her real name), who also taught and worked with children and youth in our church. She spent thirty years as a missionary in Korea and came back to my hometown in the late thirties after the Japanese required her and other U.S. church personnel to leave. She was retired and living on a missionary pension.

I don't remember her ever taking on Mr. Archon in any overt way. Certainly she never confronted him. She could hardly take him on and stay in that church or that town. Still, it seemed that every time Mr. Archon taught us those terribly racist things, Miss Buehl countered that teaching. And I don't know how she did it even to this day, at least not completely. I don't remember her ever saying anything explicit as a rebuttal, again, a risky move in that world. Rather, she had us sing "Yes, Jesus loves me" which she taught us in Korean. (I can still sing the song in Korean after all these years, though my pronunciation has a distinctly Southern [U.S.] accent.) But she also taught us the song

> Jesus loves the little children,
> all the children of the world.
> Red and yellow, black and white,
> they are precious in his sight.
> Jesus loves the little children of the world.

Somehow I know that the connection between the two songs is basic to Jesus' love. You don't have one without the other.

Miss Buehl also took us to her house and showed us art and artifacts from Korea. There were toy houses, beautiful dolls, intricate paintings of landscapes and people, wall hangings, and much more. It was my first experience of anything I remember outside my own culture, and Miss Buehl placed all of these things in the story of Jesus' love. To this day I do not know how I learned it, but I know that Miss Buehl was right about Jesus, and Mr. Archon was wrong about "colored people."

You see, Mr. Archon took God's story and put it in the racist story. Miss Buehl took the racist story and put it in God's story and called it fundamentally into question. I understand this to be the narrative work of the church. Without Miss Buehl's teaching and witness I have no idea what direction my life would have taken.

There may be nothing more basic than getting our stories right. Stanley Hauerwas sees as clearly as anyone how much our lives are shaped by the operative story or stories that work on us and through us.[1] The individualism in our culture often obscures how much we are shaped by the story, the history of our lives. We often see ourselves in this culture as free autonomous individuals. We fail to see that this is a story, and a false one. It conceals how profoundly we are shaped by such fictions. In the very act of seeing ourselves as free individuals, we cover up all the ways we are formed that we do not choose, including some in which we are not free at all. For example, we do not choose the times in which we live or the culture in which we are raised. We do not choose our mother tongue with the profound, inerasable imprint it has upon our thought, our feeling, and our orientation to "reality." We are by no means the free autonomous individuals of modernist, Enlightenment thought. One of the ways we, as the church, struggle against this kind of captivity is to gain greater clarity about the unfaithful stories that shape our lives and by a more self-conscious participation in God's alternative story as a different form of life. It is crucial that God's story be the formative story of the church if the church is to be the church.

In this connection Karl Barth argues that we must not locate the Christian faith in a presumed larger set of categories or some presumed more encompassing story.[2] Basic to what follows here is an attempt to keep faith with this claim. The most unfaithful and sinful betrayals of God occur precisely in those times when we place God's story in another story and attempt to make God's story serve that idol. I think here of the ways in which God's story has been placed in the narrative of slavery, or of patriarchy, or of heterosexism, or the stories of economic and political orders.

In a book concerned with rhetoric it seems especially important to be on guard against the temptation to find out what is persuasive and then bend or "translate" God's story to fit it. The notion of translation is a dangerous one. In his book *Two Hundred Years of Theology* Hendrikus Berkhof surveys the attempt by the church to translate the Christian faith into the language of the modern world, a language that becomes increasingly secular. He uses the analogy of the church as a boat navigating the river of time. But as the boat comes upon the sand banks and shallows of modernity, it has to throw out cargo in order to sail through. Such a strategy leads finally to an emptying of the vessel just to manage the obstructions of the modern, secular world and to stay afloat![3]

It is not my intent to engage in this translation strategy, for at least two reasons. One is that the secular world is in so much trouble of its own. The second is that the church needs no such strategy, and I suggest another later in this chapter. But I hope to reverse the pattern of placing God's story in the "requirements" of rhetoric and to propose the ways that rhetoric can serve the faith intrinsically.

As important as it is to get our story right, it is also critical that the concrete, material practices of our lives be intrinsic to that story.

The Practice of the Story

Peggy and I were at a party at a friend's house. They have a large living room, and I am tucked away in one corner talking to a man who works in government service. Having served in many places over the past twenty-five years he has rich experience and great stories. I love a good story, and he is plying me with one after another. He is a good storyteller, and I am having a fine time.

Suddenly his spouse starts coming in our direction. Upon noticing that she is about to join us, he enters into a practice I experience over and over again. In fact, I experience this practice so often I call it a ritual and give it a name. The name of the ritual is "Honey, I am talking to a minister, so watch what you say."

By the time she gets to us, she's got the message. She says, "So, you're a minister."

"Yes, Ma'am."

"What kind?"

"I'm a United Methodist."

"Ah, I used to be a Methodist."

"I see."

"Yes, but I'm not one anymore. Nowadays I'm into Native American spirituality."

"I see, and which tribe do you practice your Native American spirituality with?"

"What? Oh, my, I'd never do anything like that!"

"I see, then, perhaps you work with a shaman or some holy person?"

"Oh dear God, I would never do anything like that."

"I see, then, perhaps there is some group you practice your Native American spirituality with?"

"You're putting me on, aren't you? You know I wouldn't do any of those things."

"Well, what do the mean you're 'into Native American spirituality?'"

"Oh, I read a book, and I saw *Dances with Wolves.*"

This story illustrates what the scholars who study such things call "mere belief," the idea that you can engage matters of ultimate commitment and conviction merely by believing in them. Dean Hoge, Benton Johnson, and Donald Luidens call this "lay liberalism," where mainline Protestant Baby Boomers do not have "meanings," but "notions." This latter term *notions,* conveys ideas that make no demands on those who hold to them but "can be bandied back and forth like verbal playthings."[4] Mere belief seems to require little more than leisure activities like perhaps reading a book and engaging in selective offerings of pop culture.

I want to contest this as sharply as I can. I contend that if our beliefs are not embedded in practices, entire territories of our lives, what we know, what we feel, and certainly what we are committed to and convicted of will never come into play. Indeed, there are things we will never know, things we will never feel if we do not practice them. Such people are formed by some kind of practices, but they are not formed by practices around what they merely believe.

Knowing through Practices

For twenty-three years Barry Tedford was my neighbor and a good friend. During that time he worked as yard foreman in a lumber company specializing in walnut. He knows walnut with the kind of intimacy that work requires. I like to make things with walnut but on a small scale. I am not good at it or skillfully formed by long practice with it. So when I get a piece of walnut, I talk to Barry about how I intend to use it.

Barry holds the walnut board in his left hand. He licks the inside of his right thumb and then strokes the board. As he does so, he makes sounds: "Hmmm . . . hmmm . . . hmmm." Then he hands it back to me and usually says one of two things. Either he says, "Tex, all walnut is beautiful; but that piece is gonna split on you, so be careful with it." Or, "Tex, that's a beautiful piece of walnut; do something special with it."

I go back home, go into a room by myself where Peggy cannot hear me. I hold the board in my left hand. I lick the inside of my right thumb. I rub that board, and I make sounds: "Hmm . . . hmm . . . hmm." You know what happens? Not a blooming thing!

I do not have the kind of long practice and intimacy with walnut that Barry does. There are things I simply cannot know apart from that kind of engagement over a long time. One of the problems with mere belief, with only having "notions" about ultimate issues, is that precisely this kind of formation in the faith does not occur. I am not arguing works righteousness here. God's grace calls us into a new way of life and empowers us in a new range of practices. We can, however, refuse that call and turn away from the practices of worship, prayer, Eucharist, ministry, justice, and peace. Indeed, most people do.

Practice and the Formation of Feeling

A word about feeling and commitment is in order. I notice an interesting relationship between the practices of intimacy and the emotional richness and faithfulness of a marriage relationship. Good marriages require intimate practices. Take kissing for example. Kissing when you leave home, kissing when you come home, and kissing a lot in between are important practices of intimacy. It really helps, moreover, to kiss at some point even when you are having an argument. Some people say you shouldn't do what you don't feel. This is a miserable teaching. You kiss during an argument because you know that a lot more is going on in this relationship than the fact that you are having a disagreement. Besides, our feelings are formed in great part by our practices. I want practices that form a relationship that is far more important than what we may feel at a certain point of disagreement.

Kissing at the best times of your lives, and the worst; kissing when you are jubilant and when you are in despair; kissing in moments of triumph and in times of defeat; kissing in the face of the death of close relatives and friends: These are basic to the formation of a marriage of rich feeling and relational devotion. I see these signs on walls, usually in kitchens: "Kissing don't last; cooking do." I'll be hanged if this is true. I can always eat out. Someone says that you can kiss out too. If you kiss out, you're going to kiss off!

In part, I am using kissing as a metaphor for a host of intimate practices. Speaking the kind word, saying "I love you," touching each other as you walk past, smiling, warm looks of affection, sharing household duties, vacuuming rugs and picking up the house, indicating with a glance an intimate inside joke when with others: These are among the practices that make a couple profoundly *married*. Still, I don't want to get away from the concrete, material practice of kissing itself. In this culture, at least, when the kissing goes, something dies in the relationship. To be sure, an end to kissing can be a symptom that the marriage is already in trouble; but without it a basic practice of formation is absent. Such is the power of practices to deepen emotional life and commitment.

Practice and Transformation

One of my favorite biblical passages is Romans 12. In verse 1 Paul tells us to present our bodies "as a living sacrifice, holy and acceptable to God, which is your spiritual worship." Then comes this striking teaching in verse 2: "Do not be conformed to this world, but be transformed by the renewing of your minds, so that you may discern what is the will of God—what is good and acceptable and perfect." In verses 3-8 Paul then discusses the different functions and gifts that we have in the church as Christ's Body. But I want to look more closely at verses 9-21. In this section Paul lists the practices that I read as keeping us from conformity to the world and that change who we are. In these verses Paul lays out the practices by which by God's grace we are transformed. Look at just a few of these:

> Let love be genuine; hate what is evil, hold fast to what is good. (v. 9)
> Rejoice in hope, be patient in suffering, persevere in prayer. (v. 12)

15

Contribute to the needs of the saints. (v. 13)

Extend hospitality to strangers. (v. 13)

Bless those who persecute you; bless and do not curse them. (v. 14)

Live in harmony with one another; do not be haughty, but associate with the lowly. (v. 16)

If it is possible, so far as it depends on you, live peaceably with all. (v. 18)

Beloved, never avenge yourselves, but leave room for the wrath of God. (v. 19)

Do not be overcome by evil, but overcome evil with good. (v. 21)

This is some list! Except for the Sermon on the Mount I know of no other more transforming set of practices. A friend of mine for years underwent the unfair and inaccurate attacks of a right-wing extremist. Later this man was jailed for criminal actions in behalf of his causes. Among the first people to visit him in jail was my friend. He then maintained a relationship of caring and visitation until the man's death. Practices like these refuse conformity to the world and transform people so engaged.

This practice of doing good to people who have abused him is a long-standing practice of my friend. I remember once getting excessively angry with him. I said things to him I ought not to say. I was dead wrong. What caught me completely off guard was his mild and gentle response. When I later apologized to him, his response was again gentle and conciliatory. He never held my violation of our relationship against me and never brought it up. We continue to be friends. Such formation of character is constructed by long practice. In his case I see it profoundly related to his long-time practice of nonviolence.

I do not mean to suggest by this that my friend is a doormat or one who will not speak up for what is right. Anyone who has ever debated him knows the power with which he will speak forthrightly for peace and justice and how incisive his argument is. As one who knows what it is like to be on the losing side of such encounter, I can assure you that he is no doormat!

I think, too, of Paul's instruction to practice hospitality. On November 1, 1991, an alienated Chinese post-graduate student at the University of Iowa shot and killed five University of Iowa people and himself. At Thanksgiving later that same month three women, widowed by the shooting of their professor-spouses, cooked dinner for a crowd of about fifty Chinese students.[5]

Surely it is easy for a person to take a racist turn after having a spouse killed by a student of a particular race and then to blame an entire people collectively. But these three women engaged a radically different practice of hospitality and embodied in that practice a challenge to any such racist turn.

In sum, we are formed by the practices that populate our lives. Our knowing, our feeling, and our convictions and commitments are constructed from these practices. In the church practices like those outlined by Paul in Romans 12 resist conformity to the world and transform by God's grace those who live life in the Way. To live God's story and to join practices intrinsic to that story are foundational to the life of the church.

The church also lives in a host of different cultures. How is the church to negotiate its relationship to these cultures? How does the church live God's story as alternative community in a world with different stories and with practices that are different and sometimes new. The next chapter takes up these issues.

Chapter 2

Pitching Tent

---

*The Word became flesh
and pitched tent with us.*

H ow can the church negotiate its relationship to the cultures of the world? I approach such issues from an incarnational commitment. That is, I attempt to take the Gospel of John seriously where it says "The Word became flesh and lived among us." Let us use this teaching as the way to address the relation of the church to the culture(s) in which it must address its witness.

Incarnation as Story

It is, of course, key that the church take the Word with ultimate conviction. We are the community of faith who believes that the Word of God has come into history in Jesus of Nazareth; that he is the forerunner and embodiment of God's reign; indeed, that he is the revelation of the one true God; and that in his life, death, and resurrection we see the mighty work of God in the world. In Christ the Word has become flesh.

As I work with this text in the Gospel of John, it is clear that one cannot address it finally if one does not see it as a teaching growing out of a story. Surely, this story begins in ancient Israel with the God who creates the world and engages this creation in its history, in the wanderings of Abraham and Sarah, of Isaac and Rebecca, and Jacob and Rachel, in Exodus and in promise, in prophecy and wisdom, in Exile and restoration, in

19

Temple and in synagogue. We cannot reckon with the story of Jesus apart from the story of Israel.

At the same time we cannot engage the story of Jesus apart from the story of the church. It is the church that wrote the New Testament, as the people of the God of Israel wrote the Hebrew Scriptures. Our Gospels grow out of the life of Jesus as witnessed by the apostolic church, and as the later church attempts in its own life to proclaim what God has done in Christ, at first in Jerusalem and Galilee, later in the Hellenistic world, then across the Roman Empire, and finally "to the ends of the earth." Formed from the life, death, and resurrection of Jesus, the church was born at Pentecost and in the power of the Spirit becomes a living story across the two thousand years since.

This story is necessary to our understanding of the Incarnation.

I contend that this story is the true story of the world. I say this in spite of popular views to the contrary. I heard someone say recently, to the affirmation of those gathered, that the great religions of the world are all equally true. I resist such notions thoroughly. First of all, I don't know how anyone would know such a thing. Who has engaged all the world's great religions in such depth as to know what truth is embodied in their traditions? When I say *engaged,* I mean who has practiced all these in such intrinsic ways as to be able to make such an extraordinary claim. We cannot be on all those paths at once.

Moreover, what is to be done with all the ways that the world's religions disagree sharply with each other? To say that such are equally true is to indicate that one does not know very much about their substantive convictions.

In parentheses, I have another suspicion about claims that contend that all the world's great religions are equally true. If all the religions of the world are equally true, how does such a notion operate in the U.S. American context? I maintain that it functions to turn faiths into commitments of privacy: My view becomes my individualistic view, which I can hold in my private and personal life but not in the larger community. The result is that the story of the nation state then becomes the story of all the great religions because it makes it possible for these religions to flourish in private life, and we all owe the state for ending the competition of these entities with their "endless conflicts."

The result is that the story of the nation state then becomes the "real" story. Christian faith and other religious traditions are then peripheralized, individualized, privatized, and subservient to the nation state, or relegated to a kind of pop psychological realm to provide us with nonaddictive personalities and to generate motivation to fight the nation's wars and to work for a living in a consumerist, secular order. As Stanley Hauerwas never tires of asking: "Whose story is working through you?"[1] My hope in this book is that we as Christians can approach U.S. culture with a story formed by the faith and not by the nation state or a consumerist economy.

Please understand, it is not my wish as a Christian to deny that God is at work in other religions of the world. Surely God is. If one believes, as I do, that the story of the world is that of a Triune God who creates and redeems the world and who will finally take it to its completion, then nothing and no one can keep such a God out of any part of the world, including the enclaves of atheism here and about. For this reason—if for no other reason, and there are other reasons—the church will listen respectfully to the views of others. We never know ahead of time what God is saying to us through the other. Further, in the world of the Christian story those of other religions and of no religion are children of God and people for whom Christ defeated the powers on the cross. In these terms the sources of Christian hospitality and its imperatives are Infinite.

Finally, nothing is to be construed here as some underhanded attempt to gain ideological advantage over other religious commitments. The Christian commitment is to persuasion, not to

21

coercion. It is a violation of the mission of the church itself to attempt to control people through coercive means, that is, to attempt to convert other religious devotees through manipulation or any form of force. We serve a nonviolent Savior; the church must give up on coercion.[2] I hasten to add that there are few things more devastating to the witness of the church than its violations of others in "the name of Christ."

The Unsecular World

Having said these things, then, I want to return to the Incarnation and its relationship to the world. Some frame the matter by saying that Christ has entered the world and the issue has become one of how to make Christ relevant to the world or how the good news of Christ can be mediated to the world. I want to maintain instead that God's story is not a mere entrant into the world; it is the story of the world itself so that the world cannot be understood rightly except in terms of the story of God. When Christ enters the world, the world is changed, history is changed, the powers are defeated on the cross, and their ultimate fate is clear.

This is very important to understand today because of much that one finds happening in the literature and advice on church growth and congregational development. This literature is filled with notions of making the faith relevant or mediating the faith to the world. I believe this to be a theological mistake. No doubt I have done my share of this, but I have more recently also tried to redress such an approach. My focus on the metaphor of pitching tent is my attempt to offer an alternative to such approaches, one that is in concert with the biblical story and a faithful continuation of church tradition. Such an approach can learn from "the world"; but the world now is understood from within the Christian story, not seen as some secular entity to which we must somehow become connected.

22

To put it another way, when "the Word became flesh," this was not an instance of God joining a world not God's. It is rather the revelation not only of who God is but who and whose the world is. The world is then not a secular order to which God must become relevant but the creation of God, fallen but to be redeemed and completed in God's ultimate victory over sin, evil, and death. So the job then is not to get relevant to the world but to enable the world to see itself for what it is and ultimately will be. Or to say it one more way, the job is not to get God's story into the world but to place the world in God's story.

Obviously, the church's story is not the only story out there. In fact, its story is dimly heard in comparison with the din of the American story and the capitalist story, to be redundant, though these two are hardly the only narratives, even if they are the dominant ones. Moreover, it is not a question of Christ and culture or of the church and culture. There is no culture-free mediation of Christ, and the church always takes on at least some of the cultural practices of the world where it happens. I will not contend for a culturally invisible form or for some vacuous ideal of the church, both abstractions if there are any. Rather I want to argue for the church as a culture (following Hauerwas), but one among cultures. There has never been a case of the church in its concrete storied tradition when it is not also a part of some specific, historical culture(s).[3] The focus here, therefore, is to exhort the church to be an alternative culture that indeed participates in yet other cultures as within God's world. The important question is how this can be faithfully done.

The church does not float above the ground like some eerie phantom. Rather as an alternative culture it must continually negotiate its relationship to the cultures it encounters. One thing is clear. This is not withdrawal. The world is God's and is beloved of God. Therefore, I make no plea for the church to retreat into some "spiritual" hovel.

In working in a culture the church must address the stories and practices and collectivities of such settings. In some places the church will be in affirmation, perhaps only pointing to such places to see them with the eyes of faith. In other cases, there will be withdrawal of the church certainly in terms of its participation in certain practices. In other settings the relationship will be a highly selective one.[4] That is, the church will choose to work quite directly with some practices even while withdrawing from and actively opposing others.

This question of the church's negotiation of its relationship to other cultures drives us back to the Incarnation. How are we to understand the relationship of the church, for example, to the practices of a culture? What have we to learn from the Incarnation in the attempt to deal with this issue?

The Word Pitches Tent

It is, of course, desperately important to the church's teaching to proclaim that "the Word became flesh." I hope this is clear from above. Yet, there is still more. The Word also "lived among us" in Jesus. The Greek word translated by "lived" is *skeenoo*, which means "to live or camp in a tent" or transitively "to pitch or inhabit a tent."[5] Eugene H. Peterson captures one meaning of this in paraphrase: "The Word became flesh and blood and moved into the neighborhood."[6] Kittel and Friedrich suggest "the eternal Word of God became present in time."[7]

At the same time, this phrase can be read in a way that takes on a very concrete character in the life and ministry of Jesus. That is, if pitching tent is an indigenous practice in the first century, it is true in a host of ways that Jesus "pitched tent" with the practices of his culture. Not only did the Word become flesh and take up habitation with us but also the Word joined the very relative and historically located practices of the first century in Palestine. One may argue that this is about Christ, not the church, but if the church is the Body of Christ, it seems to me that the church is instructed by this central claim of the Incarnation.

I am convinced that we find here in the ministry of Jesus the central clue to how the church as a culture negotiates its way in relationship to the other cultures in which it finds itself. The church is the Body of Christ in the world. Our mission is to be the community that embodies the Word of God in Christ in history and in the world. To negotiate our relation to the world around us requires that we take the ministry of Jesus with the utmost seriousness. To do so, several things can appropriately be said.

First and foremost, Jesus was a faithful Jew. His acquaintance with the Torah; the centrality of and his attendance at synagogue and Temple; his life of prayer and retreat; his participation in the religious festivals and feasts of first century Judaism; his identification with the story of the patriarchal families, of Moses, Elijah, and Elisha; and his conversations and teaching in the tradition of his people: All of these and more speak to his joining the religious practices of his people and their historic faith. While I shall speak later to his challenge to his tradition, for the moment it is clear that he indeed did pitch tent with the religious life of his time.[8]

Second, Jesus not only inhabits the language of his time, he inhabits a vernacular. He speaks Aramaic. To inhabit a language is to reside in a reality because language is so central to the construction of the forms of life in which we live. At the same time it is important to realize that to inhabit a language is to take up an enormous range of practices. In a culture, language is embedded in an inexhaustible—in human terms—range of practices.[9] Moreover, to inhabit a vernacular is to join the practices all the more specifically and concretely with a people. So to say that Jesus inhabits the vernacular of Aramaic is to say that he pitched tent in a profound sense. To say that Christ is fully human is to say no less.

The importance of inhabiting a language can perhaps be seen best in a negative example. Chinua Achebe's great novel, *Things Fall Apart*, has never been translated into the native Igbo language of Nigeria. Achebe tells this story. When the Christian Missionary Society worked on translating the Bible into Igbo, they brought together six converts. But each came from a different area and each spoke a different dialect. As they worked their way through the biblical text, each of the converts offered a translation. Not surprisingly, the resulting "collage" is unlike any one of the six dialects. "Yet, this 'Union Igbo,' as it is called, authorized by repeated editions of the Bible, became the official written form of the language, a strange hodge-podge with no linguistic elegance, natural rhythm or oral authenticity." Achebe reports that his grand father was one of the earliest converts in Nigeria; and his father, an evangelist and teacher, loved "Union Igbo." "He considered it a work of the Holy Spirit." But Achebe considers it unfit for literature: "There is not one great book written in that dialect to this day." Susan Gallagher concludes: "Consequently, one of the world's great novels, which has been translated into more than thirty languages, is unable to appear in the language of the very culture that it celebrates and mourns. This irony seems an apt symbol for the complex ways Western Christianity has both blessed and marred the cultures of Africa."[10]

Third, Jesus not only inhabits a vernacular, he inhabits a vast cultural form of communication. That is, Jesus made his ministry with the marginal people of his time. They were primarily illiterate and therefore made up of people who engage the world through the practices of an oral culture. For example, storytelling is a fundamental practice in oral culture, and from what we read in the Synoptic Gospels Jesus teaches in the story form of parable.[11]

Fourth, he is the son of a carpenter and takes on the same occupation as his father. Certainly he engages in economic practices of some kind. Further, his teaching and the location of his ministry suggest more than an abstract acquaintance with vineyards and wine, the sowing of grain, the herding of sheep, fishing, the tending and caring of trees, and, yes, even the paying of taxes, among others. Such activities are highly specific and particular to his time. In these things he is, again, fully human.

So far, however, it may seem that Jesus is merely complying with and accommodating himself to the culture and the practices of his time. This, of course, is sharply mistaken. New wine is not to be put in old wineskins. As faithful as he is to his religious tradition, he nevertheless calls consistently into question the purity code and the purity practices of his time. He repeatedly violates the boundaries drawn to separate impure people from the righteous. He even declares that he is called to "sinners," not to the righteous.

In his encounters with people the purity code is constantly broken. His encounter with the Gerasene demoniac is a good example. The demoniac has an unclean spirit—his name is legion, he is crazy, and therefore impure. He lives in a graveyard, a very impure place. There are swine nearby, very unclean creatures. It is hard to conjure any place more impure than this, yet this becomes the site of healing by Jesus. Another example comes from Walter Wink who points out that every time Jesus engages women in the Gospels, he violates "the mores of his time."[12]

In terms of his teaching, a basic key to the exegesis of Jesus' parables is to see the myriads of ways the purity code is challenged and called into question. It is the good *Samaritan,* the *prodigal* son, the *publican,* and a host of other people and figures who display the barrenness of the tradition of purity. One parable separates those who refuse the great banquet from those with all sorts of impurities—read disabilities and needs—who are included. His "violations" of the Sabbath by act and teaching are one more instance of his challenge to the tradition of his time.

So by any defensible account Jesus certainly does counter, refute, actively teach against, and in general violate the code of purity of his time. So that if he did "pitch tent" with the practices of his time, he also radically opposed central activities of his tradition; and his life and teaching are subversive of a major dimension of his culture. No attempt to work with "pitching tent" as a metaphor can ignore this crucial resistance in the story.

Incarnation, the Story of Jesus, and the Story of the Church

What implication does this have for the church? If the church is a part of a story, then how is the church to relate itself to the story of Jesus and his pitching tent with some practices of his culture but actively opposing others?

First, we must resist any attempt to schematize the story of Jesus so that we come up with a set of "rules" for pitching tent or some "recipe." John Milbank suggests that if we see a "pattern" in the stories of Jesus in which Jesus is the Incarnate Word of God, for example, the stories must not be "reduced" to this pattern in such a way that the *idea* of Incarnation takes the place of the complexities of the stories. When the stories are reduced to a pattern—especially one overly specified in doctrine—they become rigid, too vulnerable to accommodation, less open to revision, and lose the vitality stories have to provide an account of who Jesus is.[13]

At the same time the claim that Jesus is the enfleshed Word of God always "exceeds" the stories, that is, none of the stories individually nor all the stories in sum "add up" to Jesus as Incarnate Word. Yet, "this idea is an inseparable part of historical Christianity, and such speculations are unavoidable, though they may remain ungrounded."[14] My point is that we will inevitably use this pattern, but that we cannot "reduce" the reality of the Incarnation to this pattern.

A second implication is to see the Incarnation and the stories of Jesus as part of the larger story of what God has done, is doing, and will do. Milbank contends: "We do not relate to the story of Christ by schematically applying its categories to the empirical content of whatever we encounter. Instead, we interpret this narrative in *a response which inserts us into a narrative relation to the 'original' story*."[15] That is, the church stands in a relationship to Jesus and the Gospels "*within a story that [includes] both*."

Specifically, Jesus' mission cannot be separated from his teaching on the reign of God and the establishment of the church. We respond to Christ by incorporation into this new community, a community founded in Christ and empowered by the Holy Spirit. Milbank states: the story is "*not* just the story of Jesus, it is the continuing story of the Church, already realized in a finally exemplary way by Christ, yet still to be realized universally, in harmony with Christ, and yet *differently,* by all generations of Christians."[16] So we can say the stories of Jesus are part of a larger story that begins in creation, continues in the story of ancient Israel, finds its messianic and salvific clarity and event in Christ, and by the power of the Holy Spirit establishes the church and its ongoing life.

Third, it is central to "pay attention to the play between" pattern and story.[17] I mean this in two ways. In one sense, we must not neglect the play between the idea of Incarnation and the stories of Jesus in the Gospels. I think here of interpretations of Jesus that through "realized eschatology" or "interim ethics" or "materialist readings," or "liminality," or reductions of "the historical Jesus to his probable language" make the stories incidental or actively reconfigure them into a scheme that denies and/or obscures and/or restrictively formulates their narrative detail. It is necessary to move back and forth between the idea of the Incarnation and the stories. The idea demands a return to the story and the story to its interpretation. "The idea helps to confirm *that* God is love, the narrative alone instructs about *what* love is."[18]

In another but related sense, we in the church and its story find ourselves also in the tension and the play of the pattern and the stories of Jesus. That is, we live in a radically different culture than that of the first century in which Jesus lived. This means that we do not simply repeat what Jesus does. Repetition of his acts in the full-blown context of that culture is not available to us. Yet, we ignore the rich stories of his life, death and resurrection at our peril. We live in a narrative relation to the stories of Jesus and our understanding of him as the Word made flesh.

A friend of mine we'll call Tom in Phoenix, Arizona, where I live, is hard at work in his home one day attempting to meet a deadline. The doorbell interrupts his work and upon opening the door, he is confronted by a seventeen-year-old young woman who wants to use his phone to call her family. "Something is wrong with my car. It smells funny and the back tire looks flat." Reaching her home, she finds no one is there but her mother who is coming over. Tom wants now to get rid of her. He is busy, but it is 108 degrees outside, and the good Samaritan story pops up into his mind. Under his breath he curses that he would remember that story at a time like this. He says to her that perhaps he needs to look at the car, which is around the corner. Once there he discovers that the car does have a flat, that the young woman has not ever had a flat, does not know how to fix one, and does not know whether she has a spare or a jack. Tom cannot get the good Samaritan out of his mind, so he asks her to open the trunk to see if she has spare and jack. She does. He feels he should not wait to see if the mother can fix it, but that he will because this is what Jesus would have him do. He remembers a sermon to the effect that when Jesus says to love your neighbor, it means the next neighbor you meet who is in need. He does not have time to fix this flat, but he cannot get the stories and teachings of Jesus out of his mind as he deals with the young woman.

Note some things. Tom does not know what a Samaritan is, but he is not one. He just knows that they are regarded negatively in Jesus' time. The young woman is Hispanic, not a first-century Jew. She has a flat tire on an automobile; it is not a camel or a donkey with a bad hoof. Tom has no training even to begin to describe in general detail the culture in which Jesus did his ministry. In this situation he is not dealing with someone who has been attacked by robbers and left to die. He does not take her to an inn where she can receive further help. He just fixes her tire and when her mother arrives, who is not friendly but eyes him suspiciously, he offers weak advice that the spare is only a temporary tire and that the flat one is ruined. Within a minute after he gets the spare on the hub and puts the jack back in the trunk, the young woman thanks him, and she and her mother get in their cars and leave.

This is hardly an exact replication of the good Samaritan story. But Tom does what he does because of this parable of Jesus. He sees himself in continuity with the stories and teaching of Jesus. We may wish that he do more Bible study; but he is, as understood here, in a narrative relationship to the Gospels.

Again, in events like this we can never replicate exactly the stories of Jesus in our own time because of the vast differences in that culture and our own. Yet in faithful instantiations of those stories, we can do what John Milbank calls "repetition with variation."[19] The fixing of a tire is not the same as the good Samaritan helping a man robbed and beaten; but there is clearly repetition in the variation, especially around the virtue of charity, for example. In an important sense this is a re-narrating of the story of Jesus. But it is not only a telling of the story; it is an enactment of the story. It is a performance of the story. It is a doing. In this sense it is a reminder that the Christian faith is not mere belief or only a society of storytellers; it is a Way. It is a culture and a community. It is a form of life and a tradition. It is a living of the story: "the ceaseless re-narrating and 'explaining' of human history under the sign of the cross."[20]

Pitching Tent in an Electronic Culture

This last point has special importance in the ways that the church negotiates its relationship with the cultures and the practices it encounters. I think here of the rise of electronic culture especially in the last century or so. The church encounters a culture and practices never addressed by the church before. The issue becomes one of placing those stories in the Christian story to be sure; it also means that the church faces the task of embodying the gospel in practices never before engaged by the church. If the church, for example, simply takes a utilitarian and consumerist approach and attempts merely to fit in with the culture, then the church abandons its story in an accommodationist move. To turn the story of the good news of God in Christ into a commodity advanced through marketing techniques is a violation of the first order. A faithful repetition of the story with variation is required in the culture forming rapidly around us, one that selectively joins the practices of the emerging culture but also that finds itself in direct opposition and resistance to many of the activities arising from these emerging forms of life.

Fourth and finally, I hope it is clear that I do not see all this as merely the work of individuals. My story about Tom may convey that I see the faith in such personal terms too exclusively. I do not. As Christians we do not participate in a story abstractly conceived; our story is that of the church, an embodied, historical concrete community of people. In this community we are called to be an alternative people, a "contrast society."[21]

This means that we not only place the world in God's story but that we address such matters as the people of God, not seeking to make the church "relevant" but to do the careful work both of how we pitch tent with the indigenous practices of a culture, on the one hand, but also why, what, and how we must oppose practices within that same culture. The church will join selectively indigenous practices but also develop deep resistance to others. Such work cannot be done by a series of guru-led experience-seekers introspecting in the spiritual enclaves of this country pursuing what "feels right," or what "fits my needs," or "floats my boat," but by a community that develops its own culture with which to love and oppose "the world."

Such a church realizes that one cannot merely trust "experience" because our experience is so profoundly formed by the culture and history in which we live. Here I mean, as just a few examples, the ways that our experience is formed of sexism, racism, classism, heterosexism, idolatry of the nation, and the consumerist formation of our economic and social lives.

Furthermore, the church defended here knows that one cannot merely "pursue one's desires" because our desires are always already socially constructed as well. When the church is understood as a concrete, lived community of the story of God, one then knows how much our experience and our desires are formed and shaped by the practices of faithful living. This is necessarily what it means for the church to be a culture.

Michel Foucault's work demonstrates how desire can function as the servant of dominating power, indicating by such a claim that such power attempts to rule, at least in part, by configuring desire in people to serve its aims. This is not an external imposition of desire forced on people but the encoding of desire consonant with the aims of power so that people want what power requires.[22]

Such desire is generated, for example, in the rituals of the nation state. The calendar year is organized in terms of the holidays and deadlines of the state, so that people "breathe" the time of the nation state. The flag is honored in ways that make it "sacred." A host of rituals such as singing national anthems, parades, and ceremonies instill patriotism and construct desire. Along with these come the apotheosis of the nation state and the glorification of its military.

Yet, a further word, we are not mere Americans who draw spiritual motivation from Christianity to serve our country. The larger reality for us is not the state but the church. Our hope is not democracy but the reign of God. Our reason to care about others is not because "all are created equal" in that inadequate abstraction from the Declaration of Independence, but because others have infinite value from the God who created the world and who became human and crucified for our sake. We live not in some hope of "ongoing progress" but in the promises of God who will never let us go.

I want to be clear here. I do love my country. Not to do so is to have an inadequate theology of culture. Love of country, however, is a difficult thing for Christians to do rightly. To love one's country as a Christian requires that we place our country in God's story, not the other way around. I do not mean that the church is to seek to be the "official religion" of the nation state. We must not accord the state that kind of authority and theological legitimation.

It should be clear that I have a much greater problem with the state than with my country. For example, I see this country as its wonderfully complex array of people, as the breathtaking beauty of the land, and as the place where the stories of our lives are lived out, among many other things. In terms of the nation state, I find William Cavanaugh's characterization quite helpful. He argues that we should treat the nation state like the telephone company. That is, it is a large bureaucracy that always promises more than it can deliver. Among Cavanaugh's concerns is the way the nation state absorbs other stories into its own and the way that it uses war to mobilize support for its state-serving aims.[23] Hence we can love country but see the state in far more utilitarian terms. It is certainly not to be made "sacred" or given any kind of ultimate significance. Treating it like the telephone company is a good idea. Further, the church is to be a contrast community to the state. Therefore, negotiation of the relation with the state is a continuing challenge to the church. Finally, I do not mean to suggest that Christians cannot be active citizens in the state. We can, indeed, fulfill the role of citizenship as people devoted to the good of the kingdom of God and work in these terms in behalf of the common good. We do not withdraw from the political process but we do participate in it on very different grounds.

Summary and Conclusion

To sum up, an incarnational approach to the relationship of the church as a culture in the cultures of the United States in the twenty-first century involves six "moves."

1. The Incarnation is the story of God, the God who creates the world, discloses Self in ancient Israel, comes to redeem the world through the enfleshment of the Word in Jesus Christ, and who continues to work through the Holy Spirit and the church.

2. This story makes God's story the story of the world. To understand the world aright is to place the world in that story. It is the responsibility of the church to witness to the world as to who it is. This story redefines the world and reconstrues the context in which the church does its work.

3. The Word pitches tent in the world, taking up habitation with the world and joining the indigenous practices of that time and place.

4. Jesus as the Word not only joins the practices of that world but also directly opposes central practices of his time. So that the church as the Body of Christ not only joins indigenous practices in the cultures of today but also finds itself in opposition to certain cultural practices in order to be faithful to Christ.

5. The church maintains a constant interplay between the idea of the Incarnation and the life and teaching of Jesus in the Gospels so that neither the claim that Jesus is the Word made flesh nor the concrete display of his life, teaching, death, and resurrection are separated.

6. The church is in a narrative relation to the stories of Jesus, one in which we "repeat" those stories but in a variation that addresses the ongoing story of God's world with its distinctively different forms of life and practices.

This response to the Word Incarnate is the approach with which I address the emerging culture and the matter of persuasion as it takes on a multisensory and multimedia character. It is not my intent to place God's story in these persuasive practices, but to place these practices in God's story. That is, my intent is to ask how these practices serve God's story, not how the church can be more relevant to this culture. These things I will attempt to do as one within the church as an alternative community in this culture. Such a stance requires that the church not only pitch tent, but that the community of faith discover new ways to do prophetic witness as well. To begin we look at the new form of rhetoric practiced in electronic and digital culture. This is the concern of the next section.

Part Two

Rhetoric in Image, Sound, Beat, Light, Move and Dance

Chapter 3

Multisensory, Multimedia Rhetoric

Today the word *rhetoric* has a bad reputation. Often it means overblown language, or a style bankrupt in thought, flourish without substance. It can mean the kind of talk that comes from people who don't know much, and don't seem to mind, but who have "exalted" means of presentation for superficial and trivial ends.

It also means manipulation. It suggests someone who knows all of the buttons to push to advance a point of view and/or a set of self-serving interests. It involves trickery, gimmicks, the wily uses of indirection, and the ploys of high emotion to serve hidden aims. It conceals the ways that moral commitments are evaded or violated.

For good reason we need to be wary of rhetoric as a science of manipulation. Never in the history of the world has as much time, money, people power, research, and meticulous attention to detail been given to manipulation as in advertising. The use of "hidden persuaders" is now simply the mode of operation in commodity promotion.

In Phoenix one of our tire companies has a TV ad promoting their wares in which they make the point that you can return one of their tires at any time. The ad portrays a woman in her seventies bringing a tire back and throwing it through one of the large plate glass windows of one of their stores, complete with the name of the tire company on the window. The ad nowhere indicates that this is an inappropriate or illegal act or immoral conduct. One can view the ad as the way to return a tire to this company.

The ad works. I cannot forget the name of the company, and I always remember I can bring the tires back. Yet, I wonder what happens to a customer who brings a tire back and throws it through a window. I doubt that the "rhetorical move" in the ad is acceptable consumer action to the tire company. It would be interesting to see what a judge in a court of law would do with this kind of false but effective advertising.

Forms of manipulative rhetoric certainly exist. In this chapter, however, I argue for a different use of rhetoric. Rhetoric can, indeed, serve the faith in intrinsic ways. It can serve God's story. So we turn to a distinction between rhetoric as immoral manipulation and rhetoric as a faithful use of persuasion.

Rhetoric: Immoral Manipulation or Ethical Persuasion

Rhetoric has a checkered tradition. In Plato's dialogue *Gorgias*, he denies that rhetoric is an appropriate discipline for political life. It is not an art but rather a form of flattery and a sham correlate of justice. Lacking a subject matter of its own, rhetoric has no truth to display, but rather deals in belief and illusion, not with knowledge. Rhetoric is a realm of tricks, of deceit, of unethical practices, and of surface triviality. Even in *Gorgias*, however, Plato recognizes that there can be a true rhetoric; but it is in *Phaedrus* where he addresses a true practice of persuasion. Here rhetorical technique must be intrinsic to its subject matter. While rhetoric is a means, the means employed is to embody and serve the truth and the good. The rhetoric must be consistent with and cohere in the truth and the good. For Plato this requires education in philosophy.

Aristotle challenges Plato's more negative views of rhetoric.[1] He sees the necessity of rhetoric as a tool, arguing that those who speak the truth and do so justly have an obligation to be persuasive. Too many things, moreover, are not known in a way that they can be demonstrated absolutely. Thus persuasion is necessary in those areas where we know only probabilities and not certainties. While wrongful uses can be made of rhetoric, any good thing can be misused, claims Aristotle. Sophistry does not inhere in the faculty of speaking as such, but in the moral aims of the one speaking. For Aristotle, then, rhetoric is the discovery of available means of moral persuasion in each case of its use.

Debates over rhetoric continue throughout Western history, but Plato and Aristotle frame the issue as it will continue to be addressed. In the modern period critiques of rhetoric tend to stress commitment to truth and rigorous honesty in intellectual endeavors. The stress is on depth of insight and a thoroughgoing attention to consistency of argument and to communication without ornamentation. Along with this is a deep suspicion of rhetorical trickery. High sounding verbal repertoires are distrusted. The impatience with the pompous, the disdain of the trivial, and the sharp critique of achieving ends through any means necessary fuel the critical fire of many modern thinkers.

Yet, surely, this dualism of a high-minded modernist commitment to rigorous thought and communication without deception and a rhetoric of devious techniques and trivial dexterity is not adequate to examine what is before us here. First of all, modern philosophy cannot claim such high ground for itself! And rhetoric cannot be reduced to the elevated claims of a snake oil salesman.

Calvin: Rhetoric as "Accommodation"

We need a construction of rhetoric that is alternative to both of these polarities. I find William Placher's reading of Calvin's understanding of rhetoric to be quite helpful. Placher

41

states that if rhetoric is "tricks and flashy gimmicks, then Calvin was against it." Yet, Calvin's theology in a more substantive sense was "thoroughly 'rhetorical.'" Calvin does not expect his readers to grasp everything about the Christian faith—no one does—but he wants them to secure "the right sensibility, and attitudes and act in the right way." For Calvin true knowledge of God comes not from empty speculation, but from "that which will be sound and fruitful if we duly perceive it, and it takes root in the heart."[2]

For Calvin rhetoric moves us to act, to live our lives in certain ways, to obey God. Hence in Calvin there is a combination of the philosopher and the rhetorician. In the first he lived logic and systematics; in rhetoric he was "inclined to celebrate the paradoxes and mystery at the heart of existence."[3]

With Calvin it is not enough to be able to get something said; it is necessary to get it heard. Knowing the audience, therefore, is key to a persuasive speaker. This means a speaker must "accommodate" himself or herself to the knowledge and beliefs of an audience. To be heard a speaker cannot argue from premises an audience rejects or does not grasp. To do so invites communicative disaster.[4]

Calvin amplifies this point in terms of God's revelation to us: "God cannot be comprehended by us except as far as he accommodates himself to our standard."[5] It is not Calvin's point that God lies to us, but rather talks to us in "baby talk," as a nurse might, or to make a point more simply as a teacher does to a beginning student.

Using this "principle of accommodation" he illustrates it in several contexts. For example, in those instances where the Bible seems to see the world as flat, it simply addresses such things in ways the people of that time could understand. "God speaks to us of these things according to how we perceive them, and not according to how they are."[6] Indeed, were we to see God in all the deity's glory, we would become nothing,

42

according to Calvin's view.[7] We are all as children before God. If God spoke only divine language, who would understand?[8] For Calvin all human language bears this character of accommodation, and rhetoric understood this way is basic to God's revelation.

In sum, Calvin's approach to rhetoric is to call forth feelings and new behaviors. It is the construction of new sensibilities and a formation of the heart. His use of images of God, says T. F. Torrance is *ostensive* and *persuasive*, not *descriptive*. That is, they are ostensive in that "they point us toward God" and persuasive in that they aid us in developing sensibilities of "humility and obedience before God," but they are not descriptive as in some account of God's nature.[9]

Rhetoric as Edification

With the warnings of Plato and the instruction of Aristotle and Calvin, we can move to an alternative rhetoric, one at work in an alternative community. I contend that rhetoric is not predestined to manipulation but can be a practice of edification, of building up a community, the church. Such rhetoric can be intrinsic to the ends of the church. In such rhetoric, the faith of the church is not violated in the persuasive means employed, but rather the forms of persuasion cohere in and with the faith. My descriptions of this rhetoric seek to avoid manipulation, to avoid style and appeal without substance, and to reject the ruse of misdirection as a means to serve unstated and illegitimate communal ends.

The Emergence of a New Form of Rhetoric

An alternative construction of rhetoric must face the challenge of radically new communicative formations. The emergence of a pervasive, powerful new form of informational

43

technology and electronic culture is rapidly changing the practices of rhetoric itself, both those of a manipulative sort and those that are edifying.

Broadly speaking, human communication formations can be seen as three kinds. The first formation is that of a primal oral culture, communication in a society without a written language. The second is the emergence of writing and later print as basic characteristics of literate culture. The third is the highly technological communication of an electronic age. Manuel Castells maintains that "a technological transformation" is occurring now "that for the first time in history integrates into the same system the written, oral, and audio-visual modalities of human communication."[10] Castells describes this third formation as a culture of "real virtuality":

> It is a system in which reality itself (that is, people's material/symbolic existence) is entirely captured, fully immersed in a virtual image setting, in the world of make believe, in which appearances are not just on the screen through which experience is communicated, but they become the experience.[11]

In making a claim like this Castells realizes that our experience and our understandings of "reality" are mediated. He says: "When the critics of electronic media argue that the new symbolic environment does not represent 'reality,' they implicitly refer to an absurdly primitive notion of 'uncoded' real experience that never existed."[12]

I find Castells's claim overstated, when he says that "reality itself . . . is entirely captured, fully immersed in a virtual image setting, in the world of make believe. . . . " Yet, there is no question of the magnitude of change now in place, especially in the concrete practices of our lives. In the process these practices reconfigure and change us! This is not a change in our activity alone but in our sensibilities, in the ways we know, in the structure of our feelings, in the patterning of our desires, and even in the kinesthetic encoding of our bodies. New constructions of human life follow in the wake of these enormous technological shifts and in the rise of an array of formative practices.

Sut Jhally claims that "the visual image-system" has taken over dimensions of our lives that used to be mainly, "though not solely," defined by hearing and other kinds of perceptual experience. For example, we not only hear and see a rock band, but engage them with big screens in settings of a more multimedia kind.[13] Jhally addresses the impact of images and these kinds of settings on the basic ways we perceive and on the new "forms of consciousness" that are arising. For good reason he is concerned about the impact of these on a number of issues such as gender identity, electoral politics, children's play, and this visual takeover itself.

In his perceptive and stinging critique of the visual image-system, however, he directs his attention to Stuart Ewen's thought where Ewen maintains that the new media force a dominance of "surface" approaches over those of "substance," that is, where style can be more important than the substance of what is being communicated. Ewen claims:

> The danger is this: as the world encourages us to accept the autonomy of images, "the given facts that appear" imply that the substance is unimportant, not worth pursuing. Our own experiences are of little consequence, unless they are substantiated and validated by the world of style. . . . The dominance of surface over substance must be overcome.[14]

As critical as Jhally is of the visual image-system, he questions Ewen's polarity of a world of surface and one of substance. With Castells, Jhally argues that our understanding of reality is always socially constructed. That is, whether we live

45

in an oral culture or a print one, we do not have "direct" contact with the "real" world. Our relationships are always conditioned by the times and the cultures in which we live. In electronic culture [my term] Jhally maintains that visual images are "the dominant language of the contemporary world" and these have become "the central mode through which the modern world understands itself." That is, we increasingly engage and understand the world through these forms. For Jhally, then, the important question is not how to live outside this new culture but how to address this culture strategically.[15] I would say rhetorically.

Jhally suggests two strategies. The first strategy is one of reconstruction, that is, "to reconstruct," to learn how to do communication and to address substantive issues while working in the realm of the image-system. Or, to put this in the "language" of the Christian faith, how do we address the substantive issues of proclamation and witness so that the practices of this new "language" of the image-system serve the faith intrinsically.

The second strategy is that of learning to do analysis and persuasive critical work in this new image-system.[16] For one thing, Jhally wants to make the use of the image-system available to a much broader range of people in the society, to democratize it. This can be done, he says, by means of greater education in the use of this new "language." For example, Jhally recalls an observation by Raymond Williams that in the beginning of capitalism workers were taught how to read (so they could gain the skills to follow directions), but not how to write. So it is today, says Jhally; we are taught how to read the use of images, but not how to produce them.[17] He calls for a much greater functional literacy in the language of the image-system so that we know how to use the language and what it does. For example, we need to understand who produces advertising and what their interests are in order to resist the manipulation and control of corporate and political powers.

We also need to learn practices of production in media so as to promote substantive claims of our own.[18]

My concern with Jhally's work here is his use of the metaphors of the literate world to talk about the image-system. Note his use of *literacy* and of the *reading* of images and of his metaphor of *language*. As we shall see below, this image-system will require new metaphors. The use of those of literality distorts the character of what we *engage*; that is, we do not merely read media or "speak" with media, we view, hear, rhythmically participate, and in illuminative contexts we move and dance. Furthermore, the emphasis must not be limited to images only because of their metaphoric reference to the visual. We need a more encompassing descriptive word. For this reason I shall use the word *figure* to discuss multisensory and multimedia rhetoric.

Figure, Not Image Alone

The focus in this book, then, is on figure, not image alone. It is crucial to make this distinction. Image is too identified with the visual, and what is addressed here are multisensory and multimedia practices that are far more than the visual alone. By *image* I mean visual experience, actual or imagined. By *figure* I mean not only the visual but also the audible, rhythmic, illuminative, and kinesthetic movement and dance. I also mean taste, touch, and smell, actual or remembered or fantisized. Hence figure is the more inclusive term; the visual is a category within it. I realize that *image* is often used for what I mean by *figure*. Figure, moreover, can be used for experience that is visual. But I make a sharp distinction here to make sure that we deal with more than the visual only, and that the visual does not become a reductive or ruling "metaphor" for other sensory events.

This distinction is important as well because of the role that the visual has had in the West in knowing. Chris Jenks writes

47

of Western culture as one where the eye is central. Martin Jay characterizes the West as dominated by "a scopic regime," where our forms of knowing come primarily through visual action and metaphors of sight.[19] Think of the ways we use the visual in everyday talk: "I see what you mean." "From my point of view. . . ." "From my perspective. . . . " "As I see it. . . . " "Do you see what I mean . . . ?" Jenks is right about the centrality of the eye in Western knowing. Not that other sensory practices are absent, but these do not have the centrality of the visual.

And deeply related to the above, is the role of literate culture as it has come to prominence in the West. I am struck by how often literate practices and metaphors are used to characterize or describe the engagement of other sensory experience or multimedia events. Print practices of seeing and reading a text are so pervasive that we carry metaphors from these activities, especially in the academy, over into a host of other practices. The talk is of "reading" media or of "media literacy," or, more recently, of the role of media in "inscribing" our bodies. I understand that some of this is metaphoric, but certainly not a good deal of it. Such usage, even in metaphoric expression, reduces and impairs multimedia and multisensory experience.

Or, think of the place of the word *observation* in Western method and procedures of knowing. Jenks maintains that observation has become "a root metaphor within social and cultural research, which uses an extensive vocabulary of 'visuality.'" He contends that the word is now applied in an almost unthinking way and has become basic to the ways we attempt to relate to and understand "the concerted practices of human communities." Jenks understands these developments in social and cultural studies as "refinements of the conventional 'ocularcentrism' abroad within the wider culture."[20]

Today these visual, literate metaphors are especially involved in the work of those who characterize the "world as a text." Such characterizations come out of language studies that emerged so powerfully in the twentieth century.[21] There can be little question of the role of language in constructing the ways we perceive and know the world. At the same time, as Wittgenstein so profoundly understood, we do not know what a word means until we know how it is used. Our language is embedded in practices. The world is not a text, it is "language" embedded in "a world of practices." So that language and world are interrelated, meaning that we do not have one without the other. Our practices, moreover, are not visual alone, but engage an enormous range of sensory activity, including the audible, the rhythmic, the kinesthetic, and taste, touch, and smell among others.[22]

To describe the world as text is reductionistic, even when one suggests that it is metaphoric on a broad scale. Professionals in the academy need to be especially cautious. The occupational hazards of working so much with texts leads one to a too exclusive linguistic construction, on the one hand, and to a failure to engage adequately other sensory experience and practices, on the other.

Can we know these sensory activities apart from language? No, but we also do not understand language apart from the practices in which it is embedded. At one time in my life I worked as a laborer around cement finishers. In that job I was able to watch and listen to them talk and work. I don't ever remember any one of them trying to describe their work in representational language. That is, in getting the wet concrete in the right mixture of cement, gravel, and water they do not describe the mix in terms of highly graduated concepts of texture or moisture or density. Their language is more like: "That's too wet," or "That's too dry." "Put more water in it," or "Better throw some more gravel in that mix. It don't look right." When they begin the finish work, they talk of things like "feel," or making it "smooth" or "needing the right touch."

On those rare occasions when they gave me the trowel to "try my hand at it," their instruction was not highly technical language that attempted to help me get it right in words first. Their instruction was more like: "Hold the trowel this way." "Don't rub so hard." Or "Don't use too light a touch." They would say, "You got to get the feel of it." Or, "Do this." Their expressions of hope for me were: "You'll get the hang of it. Just keep on." These were masters of the craft. I was not even an apprentice. Yet, I remember to this day that the practice of cement finishing has no language adequate to it. To be sure it has a language, and no one can learn to do cement finishing without the use of signs; but cement finishing is not merely a text. It is a language formed around tactile and kinesthetic practices and decidedly not formed around "reading texts." It is talk embedded in a range of enormously complex skills; and what is known implicitly, while structured by signs, is decidedly more than language.

So, we must not reduce sensory experience to the visual alone. The audible, the rhythmic, the illuminative, the kinesthetic, the moving gestures of dance, the olfactive, the tactile, and taste require a greater range of sensory language. This language must not distort/obscure (as in visual metaphor), silence (as in sound and beat), darken (as in light and illumination), desensitize (as in taste and smell), or numb (as in touch) their particular practices of construction and reception. We must not miss the dance because we only *talk* the moves.

We turn, then, to a more nuanced description of major sensory expressions and practices to understand how they are used in our time. Further, we then examine what happens in the synthesizing of these in multisensory and multimedia events because the synthesis of these is far greater than the "sum" of the sensory "parts." The engagement of multisensory and multimedia experience, especially in spectacle-like events, takes on an environmental, an ecological character, one in which we are immersed. My contention is that such immersion is a radically other experience than "reading." Further, these spectacles are not merely passive spectator events. Increasingly, the crowd performs with the artist, a radically different practice. These events can indeed be used to distract us and to anesthetize us to major issues and questions that shape our very lives. But the violations of spectacle do not rule out the possibility of alternative and oppositional events and the formation of communities of resistance.

First, my turn is toward particular sensory experiences, specifically image, sound, beat, light, move, and dance. Each of these has received enormous scholarly attention and is now the focus of an even more vast literature and production by those who work in these fields. My job here is not to encompass the findings of these efforts but to lift up major characteristics of current use. This is a more appropriate task in this space, but still daunting. By coming to greater clarity about their uses we can understand better how to pitch tent with these practices but also how to use them in intrinsic service to the faith.

I understand Jhally's work as a call to a new rhetoric, one that requires a new range of practices. The practices of persuasion in the advertising industry will not do, but technological transformation and emergent electronic practices open up new dimensions of persuasion. These practices do not have to be trivial, shallow, and manipulative trickery. While most of these new forms of persuasion are to be looked upon with great suspicion, this book describes practices of rhetoric that offer constructive alternatives for the church.

These new forms of persuasion I call multisensory and multimedia rhetoric. I say *multisensory* rhetoric because the practices are employed in settings other than those of electronic media alone, but even these practices are influenced by the emergent culture. By *multimedia* rhetoric I suggest practices that emerge from media, especially the electronic synthesis of image, sound, beat, light, move, and dance. These are electronic forms of rhetoric the church has only begun to engage. It is crucial then to name and to examine these new forms in order to claim those intrinsic to the faith and to critique those that manipulate and misuse people. We begin this examination by turning first to image.

Chapter 4

Imagophobia and the Use of Images

I mages have a bad reputation in the West. Critics characterize them as emotional, and not cognitive. According to this
view, images instantiate feelings that are false to life and
form us emotionally in ways that create false consciousness.

For example, the film *Pretty Woman* tells the story of a
street prostitute played by Julia Roberts who wins the affection
and finally the "live-happily-ever-after love" of a megamillion-
aire played by Richard Gere. While I do not doubt that some
millionaires do business with prostitutes, this film is so distant
from the everyday lives of prostitutes as to be an outright fab-
rication. It is not mere fiction, it is outlandish fantasy. Further,
the emotions evoked in the film virtually obscure the entire
range of issues around prostitution and the women caught in
the trade. This is a classic case of the "feel good" movie.

Quite frankly, I am not against "feel good" movies altogether.
Enjoyment without needing always to engage things seriously
is an acceptable pastime in many cases. The problem is when
a serious issue is treated this way or when it becomes a steady
diet rather than a nonfat dessert. It then deserves the bad rap
as an emotional exercise without substance and without cognitive attention to everyday life.

The Dualism between Knowing and Feeling

The bad rap on the emotional character of images in the
West, however, goes beyond these concerns. It involves a dualism

of knowing and feeling, with the latter associated with images. As able a commentator on such matters as Nelson Goodman describes the "domineering dichotomy between the cognitive and the emotive." The cognitive is associated with substantive matters: "sensation, perception, inference, conjecture, all nerveless inspection and investigation, fact and truth"; the emotive is connected with the less important things: "pleasure, pain, interest, satisfaction, disappointment, all brainless responses, liking and loathing."

In a challenge to this dichotomy Goodman asserts that "in aesthetic experience the *emotions function cognitively*."[1] Goodman notes that we disable our knowing in art when we shut down our emotions. If we are emotionally numb, we simply miss the fuller range of response that art can evoke. I say, to engage art without emotion is not unlike feeling the vibration of music without hearing its sound.[2]

David Freedberg in his extraordinary book, *The Power of Images*, agrees with Goodman. Freedberg argues that "the chief obstacle" we have to comprehending and appreciating our response to images is "our reluctance to reinstate emotion as a part of cognition." Such resistance "runs deep, but never more so that when we talk about art."[3] Freedberg states further that:

> We who are educated look and behave in detached ways; we become high formalists, and we deny the wellsprings of the power inside and outside ourselves. We also omit those aspects of feeling and emotion that are usually left outside cognition and are considered so fine-grained and distinctive that they cannot be held by anything but the most anecdotal procedures in history.[4]

Freedberg also contends that "the two chief means" of modern engagement with images actually "enable evasion" of the impact of those very images. The one is that of "high critical talk," and the other that of reclaiming the context of the images under view. Both of these result in talk that can avoid the unkempt character of emotion.[5] To go to a deeply moving art show or film and then afterward to be subjected to someone so engaged in "criticism" of the event or so occupied with the "context" of the painter or the filmmaker is to violate one's sensibilities. This kind of intrusive talk invades a more deeply felt response and, indeed, obscures and distorts the moment. Can you imagine what it must be like to make love to someone like that?

This is not to say, of course, that there is not a central place for criticism and for attention to context. It is to say that they are not substitutes for the rich emotional engagement with images, art, and visual experience more generally, and for their cognitive power and impact in particular.

Images and Idolatry

"You shall have no other gods before me. You shall not make for yourself an idol ["a graven image" in KJV], whether in the form of anything that is in heaven above, or that is on the earth beneath, or that is in the water under the earth. You shall not bow down to them or worship them" (Exodus 20:3-5).

The second of the Ten Commandments profoundly influences Western history in its appropriation and use of images. Nicolas Poussin's painting, *The Dance Around the Golden Calf* (ca. 1634), displays this violation of the commandment against the making of false idols. The golden calf is of central prominence in the painting, and the debauchery and uncontained sensuality of false worship is displayed in the Hebrews' dance around it. David Freedberg points out that "the depiction of figures in violent movement" in dance is highly uncharacteristic of Poussin's work, and that within the limitations and restraint of his art the figures in the painting "can be said . . .

to let themselves go." The sleeve of one woman has slipped from her shoulder to "reveal the alluring expanse of her shoulder." Another woman, while calling the idolatrous people to the dance, is portrayed in a drape that has slipped to disclose much of her breast.[6] For Poussin, says Freedberg, this is salacious stuff.

Central to the painting is the figure of Aaron. Located opposite the golden calf, he is the lone figure attired in white. The color of his robe attests to his priestly status and stands in sharp contrast to the garish colors of the idolatrous dancers. With his right hand Aaron gestures toward the golden calf; with his left "he seems to point to his eyes." Freedberg asserts, "Nothing in a picture could more definitively make plain that sense by which we are undone. Through sight we fall into idolatry—and what follows is the unleashing of the other senses."[7]

This suspicion of images as giving rise to idolatry and to unleashed desire and dissolute behavior is sharply addressed in the painting. It is a recurrent issue in the West and in Christianity, and for good reason. The capacity for false worship seems boundless in the human condition and possesses a subtlety commensurate with any human endeavor. We make idols of the nation, race, family, romantic love, violence, gender, sexual orientation, class, and self, among a mass of finite pretenders to an infinite status. Central to all of these is a key role for images. I think here of the way the American flag is so often worshiped and given sacred status.

Isaiah speaks to the futility of those who make idols from gold and silver and then hire a goldsmith,

> who makes it into a god;
> then they bow down and worship!
> They lift it to their shoulders, they carry it,
> they set it in its place, and it stands there;

it cannot move from its place.
If one cries out to it, it does not answer
or save anyone from trouble. (Isaiah 46:6*b*-7)

At the same time, Isaiah's fire is directed against images as idols. It is not a condemnation of images as such. William Dyrness surely makes the correct point that the second commandment addresses false worship: "The line is drawn between God and idols, not between God and images."[8] Dyrness, moreover, argues that creation in the image of God means, not that we should worship the bearers of the image, but that we should praise the One who gave us the image in the first place (Psalms 8, 19). Furthermore, God commands people in Scripture to make objects like the tabernacle and the temple in order that God may be rightly worshiped.[9]

The distinction Dyrness makes between idols and images is important. Having lectured and conducted workshops on these things now for ten years in something like 400 events, I find that there is a kind of "demon rum" attitude about the use of images in the church and in the academy. At times throughout its history the church has tended to condemn rum itself, rather than its abuse, as evil. While this demon rum attitude toward images certainly does not characterize the entirety of the church and the academy, it is nevertheless prominent.

In this connection the distinction Jean-Luc Marion makes between idol and icon is especially helpful. An idol is something visible that exhausts and satisfies the gaze in the object's very visibility. The icon, however, is visible, yet infused with invisibility.[10] As a "super-saturated visibility" an icon is not the residence of a god but "a lure," as Robert Barron puts it, "to the cadences and rhythms of a deeper story."[11]

The iconic character of an image is not a "natural" property of the image. Images are socially and culturally constructed. What is "there in the image" is a function of its use. It is not some ahistorical essence that images possess but rather how they are socially and culturally formed and how they are used that determines their meaning.

I am deeply suspicious of the ways images are used in a commodity culture. Part of the problem here is not only the messages they teach but the formative capacities they have, especially in their ability to construct our very sensibilities. To resist such messages and such formation requires a different community of interpretation and the practices of an alternative formation. This is not, however, an alternative that excludes images, but rather one that makes a very different use of them. In the church this requires the faithful use of images in an alternative community of interpretation and formation.

Imagophobia and Repression

As we see above, the capacity of idols to arouse and incite desire is a long held concern, but the power of images to arouse and incite our passions is a more general source of our fear of them. We fear their power, their effects, their capacity to provoke passion, and their capacity for subversion. I call this fear *imagophobia*. It is not some natural fear arising from some essence in images and their relation to human nature. Imagophobia is not some ahistorical structure embedded in the human condition finding its expression in personal, social, and cultural life. Such an understanding seems to be a dimension of the "demon rum" response to images. Nevertheless, this social, cultural, historical construction of images has a powerful grip on the response to images in the West.

Basic to this construction is the need to set boundaries on images. David Freedberg names these fears especially in terms of the need to tether them:

All visual representation must be held in check . . . because of its strong ability to involve the beholder and to transcend natural law. It is dead but it can come alive; it is mute but has a presence that can move and speak; and it has such a hold on the imagination that it informs dreams and produces fancies that are adulterous.[12]

This fear of arousal leads to repression. Freedberg names any number of ways in which this repression occurs. One way is to turn images into art. Putting art in a museum or in a gallery sublimates and contains their power. Freedberg is not arguing that objects placed in a museum cannot move us deeply. Rather the point is that in a museum, by making images "art," we can more generally sanitize, formalize, distance, and contain their power. We can more effectively detach our response to images and displace their more fully orbed impact.

I think here of that person in a museum or gallery so thoroughly occupied in an intellectual exercise about a painting that he or she does not seem to "take it in" in some more engaged emotional and embodied way. It is like proposing marriage to someone while launched in a dissertation on the tradition of marital practices in the fourteenth century! It is not my point that museums and galleries are the only place such things happen, but rather that they have the capacity to institutionalize this kind of response.

Let me be clear here: I do not suggest that the intellectual response is a mediated response and that a more fully embodied one unmediated. Both are mediated responses. I am asking for a different kind of mediation, one that, while not excluding the intellectual response, also refuses to turn the intellect into a repressive dynamic, closing the door to a fuller, more engaged response.

Another form of repression is to deal with images by ranking and classifying them. The division of art into that of "high culture" and "low culture" is a tactic of ranking and classifying. It identifies "high art" with intellect, thought, and our more "cerebral" faculties. Meanwhile "low art" is the realm of the body, of emotion, of feeling, and of our "lower" faculties. This kind of "living above the sinuses" becomes a repressive way not only to approach images but also to distance oneself from their power.[13]

Yet another form of repression is to make judgments about the excellence of art. Nelson Goodman says that "Works of art are not racehorses and picking a winner is not the primary goal. . . . Estimates of excellence are among the minor aids to insight. Judging the excellence of works of art or the goodness of people is not the best way of understanding them."[14] While not questioning "that some works of art are inexplicably more beautiful than others," David Freedberg maintains that ranking devolves into "the position that assumes a radical disjunction between high and low images and high and low response."[15]

It is hardly surprising that these dynamics are heavily implicated in sexism. The patriarchal associations of men with intellect, cognition, and substance, and of women with emotion, feeling, and ornamentation pervade the Western world and certainly the world of image and art. Women are depicted as seductive and dangerous. Their threat in no small part is due to their beauty and their capacity to arouse.

When this fear of arousal is combined with beauty, the images then become subversive. Freedberg observes that when we draw from "old sources," we "know that the beautiful is dangerous and that it is wise to control it."[16] The power of image to incite desire is threat because "the eyes are channels to the other senses." Once grasped by the image, our eyes cannot withstand the captivation of emotion and feeling.[17] This power is often associated with women, and their presumed subversive capacity is characterized as a combination of image and beauty. W. J. T. Mitchell captures this sexist assessment in a summary statement: "The decorum of the arts at bottom has to do with proper sex roles. . . . Paintings, like women, are ideally silent, beautiful creatures designed for the gratification of the eye, in contrast to the sublime eloquence proper to the manly art of poetry."[18]

In sum, in the West the fear of images relates to at least three things. One is the dualism of cognition and emotion. A second is the capacity of images to arouse, and the concomitant fear that implicates them in idolatry. The third is the more general capacity of images to incite and provoke strong emotion. These, of course, by no means exhaust the apprehension associated with images in the West, but for our purposes they name basic fears as in imagophobia. They alert us not only to sources of apprehension, but also point to issues to be addressed in further reflection.

Basic Uses of Images

We need now to examine basic uses of images, especially in the contemporary setting. We will also explore the church's response as a community of formation and interpretation to each of these uses. First, it is crucial to remember that vision is a cultural achievement and that the production, use, and response to images are socially and historically constructed. We tend to think of seeing as a physical attribute alone. We do not recognize how much we have to learn in order to see. Studies show that people who were born blind or blinded very early in their lives and who have had surgical procedures to correct the physical dysfunction cannot see initially. What they see upon removal of the bandages is something like a blur of light, "a wall of brightness containing color patches that blend indistinguishably into one another." It is a "swirl of color." They have not learned to sort out this bright, colorful blur into people and objects, into distance and proximity, into the stable and the moving. Such perceptions and more must be learned.[19]

In terms of the production, use, and response to images, these arise out of social and historical circumstances and are profoundly conditioned by them. My point is that I shall not be arguing about how images *are* but will describe how they are *used*. So far as I can tell, there is no way to talk about images apart from their mediated character. We do not engage the "raw reality" of images. Our engagement with images is always already mediated by culture. Furthermore, we are at the beginning of a massive transformation in communications, a transformation that will bring different uses of images into play. We don't know what images can do in terms of these coming changes. It is wise, therefore, to speak of the ways in which they are used in the historic context in which we live.

My basic concern is how the church uses images so that it not only does not lose its soul but that its witness is intrinsic to the faith. The task is to use images in ways that serve God's story, on the one hand, and that do not get lost in an accommodation that merely apes the use of images in a consumerist economy and in the idolatries of the nation state on the other hand.

Images as Presentational

Susanne Langer makes a distinction between language and images. Language in the strict sense is "essentially discursive." That is, meaning is provided through the linear, successive "process called discourse." In this linear process words are combined to express meaning. Also, almost any word has synonyms so that we can define how we use it. Further, words can be used both connotatively and denotatively. If a word has a general connotative meaning, we can point to or use emphasis in our voices to give specific denotative meaning to it.

Images are different. Images are "wordless symbols." They are "non-discursive and untranslatable." They cannot be defined by other images and cannot "directly convey generalities." Rather, an image can be understood only in terms of "the meaning of the whole." This understanding comes through a simultaneous holistic grasp. It is therefore quite different from the linear character of discourse.[20]

I have trouble with this distinction as stated, but there is something worth preserving in the formulation. I don't know what a "wordless symbol" is, but Langer makes the important point that an image does not *tell* but rather *shows* or *presents*. For example, Collin Fry reports a comment by Georgia O'Keeffe in 1923: "I could say things with color and shapes . . . things that I had no words for."[21] Yet, even here there is language, the language of "things I had no word for"; but O'Keeffe's point is that she cannot adequately say, cannot adequately describe what she wants to convey in a painting through language. She cannot *represent* it in words, but she can *present* it in a painting. Thus the use of images comes in display and depiction.

Closely related to Langer's formulation is that of Paul Messaris who makes a distinction between discourse and the descriptive character of images. Images are "primarily a *presentational* mode of communication . . . for *representing* events rather than making propositions about them."[22] For him images are not a language, but rather are "sources of aesthetic delight, instruments of potential manipulation, [and] conveyors of *some* kinds of information."[23]

Messaris contends that while language can do analysis, the presentational character of images cannot. Analysis requires propositional claims on his view. For this reason images are not merely a difference in degree from language but a difference in kind. Pictures do not have the specialized symbols and structural properties of words necessary to define terms, to develop concepts, to build an argument, and therefore to make claims. Pictures cannot make distinctions that analysis and critique require.[24]

While I agree that images differ from words and, indeed, are a different kind of communication, Messaris' claims are too much modeled on language. That is, he discusses analysis and critique in terms of how language does them. I believe that the presentational character of images can do "analysis" and certainly "critique," but these are not done in linguistic form taken alone. In chapters 8 through 10 I argue for ways that images and figures can do a kind of "analysis" and "critique."

Finally, the practices of display and depiction with images participate in a form of life. Messaris indicates as much when he states that "the dependence of meaning on context rather than on code is a characteristic of pictures."[25] He says this in a context in which he seems to be claiming that images require context but language does not. I agree that we do not have meaningful images outside a context, but we do not have code outside of contexts either. I simply don't know what an image or language is outside a cultural context. We do not live outside contexts. Even an image that comes from a radically different culture will be received in a context in which it is seen as "strange." So far as I can tell, there are no images or codes without a context.[26]

In sum, in our culture images are used as a presentational form and, of course, differ from language in use. They do not so much *tell* as *show*, and they display things that words cannot adequately describe. Images do not do analysis and critique in the forms that language does, but I leave open the possibility of presentational forms of "analysis" and "critique" if these are not simply modeled on the ways language used alone does. Finally, context shapes our use of images and their presentational character as it does language. The best way to approach context here is in terms of story.

Images and Story

To speak of the creation and reception of images in a context necessarily involves story. I do not know how to think of context without thinking of story. We are located in history. We cannot leap outside it. Our discourse, our perceptual experience, indeed our very lives participate in stories. Stanley Hauerwas is surely right to point out that it is not a question of whether a story is operating through us, but a question of which story.[27]

Susanne Langer claims that "the first thing we do with images is to envisage a story." She believes that "Image-making is, then, the mode of our untutored thinking, and stories are its earliest product."[28] While the relationship between images and story is quite intimate, Langer has this relationship backwards. I contend that we construct and receive images in the context of a story. We understand our lives; we live out the vision for our lives on the basis of the operative narratives that tell us who we are, what we are about, and what aims we serve. I doubt that one can engage an image even in its most primal reception— meaning one's earliest developmental years—without a story. It will be, of course, a highly simple story, but a story nonetheless.

Loughlin makes the point that stories come first, before "reality." "Reality" is never without narrative. So we do "not match stories with reality," rather we "match stories with stories, or against them."[29] Images, then, as a basic expression of "reality" are received in narratives. Without narratives we do not engage them.

In Christian witness this means that the story becomes crucial as the context in which the use of images occurs. If we *buy* (and I do mean *buy*) into the consumerist story and see evangelism as some kind of commodity procedure, we accommodate ourselves to the worst uses of images. When we see people as consumers and the church's role as that of "selling" the gospel, we have left God's story. We move into the market narrative of purchase and leave the gospel narrative of gift.

Image as Icon

Images in a context also take on an iconic character. That is, images point to a host of other images, events, and experiences as part of that context. An image refers to many other things. I think here of a Jackson Pollock painting. His work is highly abstract, and much of it consists of his artful pouring of paint on a canvas placed on the floor. His work initiated a new school of abstract expressionism in the aftermath of World War II in the United States. Pollock interpreted his own work in terms of its expressive character, especially as it externalizes the turbulence of his own subjective experience. I see his paintings in the context of his life. They are iconic of his alcoholism, of his stormy relationship and marriage with the artist Lee Krasner, of his rejection of the established world, and of his resistance to any ideal or beautiful rendering of it. I cannot gaze upon his work without it "pointing to" a host of things not "in the painting."

I remember an experience with a friend. He does not know Pollock's work and has no informed acquaintance with abstract expressionism. His response is one of disdain, of wondering how anyone can see such "things" as art, and why "anyone pays money for something as worthless as all that." He then moves into some extraordinary "psychoanalytic" suggestions of Pollock's mental stability, intelligence, work ethic, and sex life! The point is my friend may not like Pollock's painting, but it certainly has iconic functions for him. While I disagree with him, I am hard-pressed to deny the "creativity" of his engagement with Pollock's work. My friend certainly sees Pollock's painting pointing to a good deal beyond the painting itself.

The iconic function of images is important, especially when images are so often demeaned in our present context. I think especially here of some literate people who condemn the use of images in contrast to reading because images "take away our creativity." They say that when they read a book that they have to imagine the people, places, and events of the plot and story line. They complain that images do this "for them," and shut down and leave undeveloped these capacities for imaginative engagement.

While I appreciate greatly the practice of reading and enjoy the imaginative work such people prize, it is a wrongheaded critique of images. *Images do not end imagination, but offer a different practice of imagination than that of reading.* Given the iconic character of images, an enormous creativity and imagination are involved in the referencing that occurs in the engagement of images.

One image can unleash myriads of events, people, places, and things. When I see an image of an oil derrick, it brings forth faces, events, machinery, and work from my five summers as a roustabout in the oil field. I imagine the tooling on the deck of the rig and the experience of pulling pipe and being drenched with water and oil. I imagine the colorful people who make up the workers on that rig because oil rigs seem to draw characters the way syrup draws flies. To suggest that images do not evoke imagination is to fail to do the close, thick description of what happens with images. To change the illustration, to argue that engaging Van Gogh's *Starry Night* fails to stir imagination is mindless.

Furthermore, in the emergent electronic and digital culture, the use of images is pervasive and is interrelated. So much of one's time is spent with cinema, television, computer, screen, and other visual contexts that these, in a sense, constitute "a world." Hence, images call forth an enormous range of other images and experiences. For example, an image of the musical group U2 sets off a torrent of experiences and fantasies. As significant as this group is for people for whom their music is truly soul, the performance and the music are triggering practices that surface thought and feeling. As we shall see below, these events typically engage fans in move and dance, improvisationally rendered. The images, thus, participate in a

67

multisensory, multimedia event that is embodied and that involves the "audience" in the performance itself. The point is these are not passive spectators but active performing audiences engaged with the on-stage artists, and images are intrinsic to this immersive experience. Engaging the iconic character of images, especially in our time, can be an enormously imaginative and creative activity.

In Christian witness, then, the iconic role of images is central to seeing the world in God's story. To whose story do the images point? What narrative becomes the referencing framework? In the "play" of referencing what context is at work? What range of images is triggered? The iconic role of image does not stifle imagination; rather it opens us to an endless referencing. In the church it speaks of a reality that can never be encompassed in image or word, but as a "super-saturated visibility," not an idol. Rather, the iconic image can be "a lure to the cadences and rhythms of a deeper story."

For example, my pastor, Jeff Procter-Murphy, recently invited Roger Strom, a potter, to throw a pot on a wheel as part of our service of worship. Clips from the videotape were then used throughout Lent. As Roger shaped the pot with his hands, he made comments that had double meaning in terms of both pottery making and the faith. In one instance he is forming a pot as it collapses on the wheel. Roger then says that sometimes he fails in forming the pot; but that if he never tried, there would be no pottery created. Roger does not then go on to make the point of how this relates to the Christian faith, but rather allows the failure to stand with this comment. Later, the "failed pot" takes on genuine beauty as it is glazed and preserved in its "collapsed state." I find it more beautiful than the other lovely pots he successfully made that day. But what strikes me is how much comment I have heard about that "failure" and its consequence and how much people draw from it in terms of its bearing on their faith and life. The "failed pot" has enormous referentiality to a host of experiences in people's lives and the way they place their own failures in the story of the Christian faith. Many also make Lenten connections between the "failure" of Jesus on the cross and then the victory of Resurrection. Images can have inexhaustible creativity in their referential capacities.

Images and the Fast-Cut Video

Fast-cut video is the relatively new use of video in which the camera shot shifts and changes every second or so and sometimes even more rapidly. In these videos the camera angle or even the scenes move quickly. TV shows like *NYPD Blue, 24,* and *Boston Public* commonly use this technique. Ridley Scott, director of *Blade Runner* and *Thelma and Louise,* maintains that the fast-cut video is the writing of the twenty-first century. Mitchell Stephens demurs; it is not a language "with a lexicon of moving images and a syntax for organizing moving images." Yet, it is a form of communication that is "in large part" not based on words. It is therefore possible that it can be "twenty-first-century writing," especially if "we're not merely trying, as André Bazin put it, to write 'in' moving images." While Stephens is certainly not uncritical of images, of what they can and cannot do, and of their misuse, he is also clear that we usually judge an innovation like fast-cut video in terms of the worst about it and esteem established modes of operation, for example, print, in terms of their best usage. We are, he maintains, at the beginning of fast-cut video. Its practice will become more sophisticated in the years to come, as well as more dangerous.[30]

Stephens describes a host of uses that fast-cut video already has. The place of music and beat in fast-cutting, the use of moving images in narrative, the collision of images, the use of disjunction and asymmetries, the crisscrossing of two or more stories, the juxtaposition of sequences of scenes, and the logic of "discontinuous peak moments": These are only a few of the practices emerging in the development of the craft of fast-cut video. These developments around fast-cut video are "structured more like music, than like prose."[31]

In 1936 in a famous essay "The Work of Art in the Age of Mechanical Reproduction," Walter Benjamin speaking of film, not of fast-cut video, says that the special art of the moving image "consists of multiple fragments which are assembled under a new law."[32] Stephens takes this as an appropriate word for where we are with fast-cut video. We are now "experimenting with these hugely promising assemblages; indeed, we have barely gotten started." The expansion and elaboration of these "new laws" has only begun.

In conclusion, we have examined some of the concerns about images: their alleged emotional character without cognitive substance, the historic and legitimate concern about their idolatrous use, and fear of their capacity to incite excessive emotion and desire. While each of these concerns can characterize a wrongful use of images, these misuses are not inherent in images as such. The "demon rum" attitude toward images does not hold up, and imagophobia is an inadequate response. Also, we have named some of the uses of images current in today's culture: the use of images as presentational modes of communication, as intimately related to narrative, as icons, and their emerging and expanding role in fast-cut video. In these uses images are not necessarily unbaptized forms. They are certainly central to multisensory and multimedia rhetoric. It is their use that determines whether they are intrinsic to faithful worship and witness, not some ineradicable essence that inexorably places them as "birthright citizens" of the fallen principalities and powers.

We now need to move to music and beat, two dimensions of multisensory and multimedia experience as important as any I shall discuss.

Chapter 5

Sound as Music and Beat

I t is difficult to exaggerate the importance of music in contemporary society. The research of Ruth Finnegan lifts up the importance of leisure in people's lives today as a corrective of those who stress a determinative role for economic factors. She finds that what people do with their leisure time—both voluntary activities and recreational pursuits—is more important than what they do for a living.[1]

Soul Music

Central to her findings is the role music plays in helping people find their "urban pathways." Music provides the most compelling narratives in their lives. Such music is what I call "soul music." By soul music I mean the music that encodes our lives and tells our story.

At fourteen I had it made. I was on the fourth string of the high school football team. (We were basically cannon fodder for the B Team.) I was also the sports editor for the eighth grade newspaper, "Behind the Eight Ball." And I was madly in love with a beautiful girl who, in but three years, would be the drum majorette of the Brookhaven High School Panther Marching Band. I have it made.

Then it begins to happen.

First, my feet go flat, and I have to get arch supports. Then my eyes go bad, and I have to get glasses. Next I notice that every

71

time I run into—notice I do not say tackle—one of those B Team running backs, I have these terrible pains in my lower spine. It gets so bad that one day I get down on the bathroom floor, cannot get up, lose control of my bodily functions, and have to wait there until my parents come home. They take me to the bone doctor, and he tells me that I have spondylolisthesis, basically a vertebra in my lower back that sits about three-eighths of an inch forward, and I have to wear a brace that goes from my hips to just under my arms. This is the temporary solution until summer when the doctor wants me to have surgery. Otherwise, he says, "You will step off a curb and be paralyzed the rest of your life." He then tells me I have to quit football, which is *the* passion of my life.

Then it gets worse. I get acne. I don't mean a few pimples. I mean the worst case of acne in all of South Mississippi. In blemishes I am Number One, and the interventions of a dermatologist do little to stop the ravages of a skin under demonic attack. Somewhere in all this I lose the girl to another football player. I feel my life is at an end.

In those years my mother wakes us every morning at 6:30 to go to school. She first turns on the radio to the country music station. The year is 1949 and Hank Williams is shooting like a star to the top of the country music world. His music brings me to consciousness many mornings. That swamp panther voice mourns out: "Hear that lonesome whippoorwill . . . sounds too blue to fly . . . the midnight train is whinin' low . . . I'm so lonesome I could cry."

Mama comes into my room. She sits down on the bed beside me, places her hand on my chest and gently shakes me. As soon as my eyes open—I am already awake—she looks down at me and says, "You are so purdy. You are so purdy." *Purdy* is prettier than *pretty* in our world. This is some claim. So get the picture: I have flat feet, bad eyes, a spine that requires an armchair back brace, and I have acne from hairline to hairline, and my mama thinks I'm purdy!

It is not hard to understand why country music is so important to me. It comes into my life from my earliest years; but
more than that, it speaks to the worst crisis of my teenage life.
It helps me "make it through the night." In the world of
Mississippi, it is impossible to grow up without it; either you
hate it or love it. While I reject it for a time, I cannot ignore it;
and I finally come to love it.

I must not fail to say, also, that later I came to see my mother's love as an expression of God's grace as well. So that in a
strange "alchemy" the crisis of my teen years, my mother's
unfailing love and the grace of God come together in the
impact of Hank Williams's music. In doing so Williams's
artistry and country music more broadly took on two ingredi-
ents I associate with soul music. First, I am encoded with it. It
forms my sensibilities. I am amazed how it crops up in the
most unexpected ways. It can appear when I least expect it,
when I am engaged in matters seemingly unrelated, and completely so, to that entire world. Country music is one of the
ways that I negotiate my life in the world. Even as a man and
one not given to the removal of leg hair with razors, I fre-
quently quote to myself the wonderful line from Deana Carter,
"Did I shave my legs for this?" Nothing so effectively speaks
my thoughts and feelings when I have carefully prepared for a
disappointing event.

To love someone and to celebrate it is to understand what
it means to say, "I'd waltz across Texas with you." Or who
encoded with country music has not been in a bad job and has
not sung with Johnny Paycheck, "Take this job and shove it!"
And what person of modest means has not sung "Too much
month at the end of the money." To be encoded with a music
is to have your sensibilities formed and significant categories of
approaching the world shaped, in part, by the music.

The relationship of the Boomer generation to rock music is
a good example of this kind of encoding. I am in a church

retreat center setting up my computer and projector and connecting to the sound system of the seminar room. As a test, I play Wilson Pickett's "In the Midnight Hour." An older Boomer walks into the room and stands there with his eyes closed and his arms straight out, just bathing in the music. At one point he shouts out to no one in particular, "I never expected to hear Wilson Pickett in a place like this!" When I inquire about his love of the song, he goes into five minutes of how the song affects him, of how it evokes his feelings and touches his life.

Country music also tells my story. In part it names the hard time of my teen years and my mother's life-sustaining love. Yet, it is more than that. The music addresses in its characteristic story forms a wide range of frustration and hope, of utter delight and deep sadness, of playful celebration and of standing up to the challenge of a world we do not have on our own terms.

Kris Kristofferson's "Help Me Make It Through the Night" is something of a hymn to me. I realize that it portrays a very sexy scene, but it addresses so much more. The song is also metaphor. It names that dark night "devoid of stars."[2] It is a prayer for help to face the shadowed times of despair and hopelessness. The heart of the song is the line: "Yesterday is dead and gone and tomorrow's out of sight." These are the reasons the song asks for help to get through a dark, lonely, desperate night.[3] I remember especially our oldest son's death on his motorcycle. In that amputational grief my prayer to God is "Help me make it through the night."

The music that encodes us and tells our story is soul music. Many genres of music, of course, operate as soul for people, and some people have more than one. My love of country is matched by my love of opera. The range of music in this society and its continuing growth and diversification open up a host of soul musics. It is likely to continue.

In the church we need far greater sensitivity to the role of soul music in people's lives. At its worst the church imposes music that is not only not the soul music of a people but is actually alien to their lives. I think here especially of classical music purists who insist on "raising the tastes" of a congregation in spite of the people's soul music. It is a form of musical colonialism. At the same time I hasten to add that contemporary praise music can equally be such an imposition.

No suggestion is made here that we do not need to do good theological work with music. We do. For example, we need sharp theological critique of classical music that embodies the "glories" of the bourgeois world just as we need critique, for example, of the inane individualism and male orientation— flaws not missing from classical music and other genres—of so much praise music. Certainly country music and other genres require such evaluation and assessment. Basic to the church's work here is the task of placing any genre of music in God's story and not the other way around. This provides opportunity for a faithful use of various genres.

Five Uses of Music

Music as the Reflection, Expression of Feeling

Music is used in many more ways as well. I can address five of them here. The first is the way that music reflects and expresses our lives, especially our emotions. Susanne Langer sees music as "a tonal analogue of emotive life." She contends that music bears "a close logical similarity to the forms of human feeling. . . ."[4] Music is not a *language* of feeling, she says, "Because its elements are not words." [She is not focusing here on lyrics.] The "vital import" of music is not semantic meaning, but "the dynamism of subjective experience":

75

Music is "significant form," and its significance is that of a symbol, a highly articulated sensuous object, which by virtue of its dynamic structure can express the forms of vital experience which language is peculiarly unfit to convey. Feeling, life, motion and emotion constitute its import. [5]

While I am unwilling to declare this the essence of music—as Langer does—it certainly is one of the powerful ways in which music is used. Further, she seems to separate language and music too much, but her work does not have the advantage of the linguistic studies of the last half-century. With these qualifications in mind there is something in her formulation worth preserving, that being the use of music to express feeling.

A central concern throughout this book is that of our formation in God's story. Basic to this, of course, is the formation of feeling. Hence the use of music in ways intrinsic to God's story is central to worship and witness. Already I have addressed the dualism of cognition and emotion in the use of images. This dualism can come into play—very strangely—in music as well. The issue in music is not whether music forms our feelings, but which feelings. In a good deal of Enlightenment thought the attempt is to preserve the "autonomous freedom of the individual" as though this is not a formation itself, and a fictitious one I might add. What we fail to see is the cultural captivity of such formations which function to sever the particular commitments of people to the traditions of their lives—like the two-thousand-year tradition of the church—and make them "cosmopolitan" members of the nation state. In opposition to this I argue for the formation of our feelings in the Christian story.

Music as Ritual Enactment

It is not enough, however, to hear music as reflecting the lives of people. Music is used for more than the representation of people's feeling. As Simon Frith argues, music, especially in performance, enacts feeling. It not only reflects but also produces feeling. Further, it not only represents but also shapes the emotional lives of its listeners.[6] Music articulates, but it also instantiates and forms us.

Frith addresses here particularly the issue of meaning and contends that the important matter is "not meaning and its interpretation." That is, the appreciation of music is not some kind of decoding. Rather, says Frith, musical appreciation is a matter of an experiential "coming together of the sensual, the emotional, and social as performance. In short, music doesn't represent values but lives them."[7] Frith quotes John Miller Chernoff's conclusion from his study of drumming in Ghana: "The aesthetic point of the exercise is not to reflect a reality which *stands behind* it but to ritualize a reality that is *within* it."[8] Frith argues that this kind of ritualization is not limited to African drumming, but is found in many genres today.

I want to emphasize this "coming together of the sensual, the emotional, and social as performance" and its capacity as a practice to enact as well as reflect feeling and life. It is central to the use of music today. Its capacity to embody feeling, to enact a form of life, to perform commitments, and to bond people makes it a powerful practice in the wider culture.

To be sure, such capacities make it dangerous. These practices can serve demonic aims, can structure violent and destructive sensibilities, can simply be at the behest of consumer capitalism, or can enact the utmost trivial banality. Obviously, these misuses deserve—require!—the sharpest kind of critique.

Yet, too much of the opposition to such events and their use of music yields the arena to its worst forms. Too little attention is given to alternative and oppositional uses of these kinds of practices. Basic to the aims of this book is to suggest different uses of these practices so that they serve Christian witness and provide alternative constructions of community. My concern is to use such practices in the service of the liturgy and of Christian prophetic critique. The use of music in the configuration of our feeling is basic to the building of an alternative community and the reconstruction of our lives in God's story.

Music as Contemplation

It would be a mistake, however, to see the use of music as related only to feeling. A good deal of the history of music, including the twentieth century, emphasizes the role of contemplation in its use.[9] No less a figure than Freud remarks that comprehension is central to his finding pleasure in art. "Whenever I cannot do this, as for instance with music, I am almost incapable of obtaining any pleasure. Some rationalistic, or perhaps analytic, turn of mind in me rebels against being moved by a thing without knowing why I am thus affected, and what it is that affects me."[10] Not many people would take a position like this on music, but the point is people do think about it.

Even the younger generations, the GenXers and the Millennials, that seem to find meaning in experience more than meaning in words still think about that experience and do, of course, use language.[11] Their search for authenticity and for the "real" are not usually oriented toward representative language in the sense of attempting to describe adequately their experience in discursive propositional language. Rather they tend to be more oriented to how the music sounds, to how it makes one feel, to a more organic taking account of the multisensory and multimedia impact of the music.

This does not mean, however, that they do not think about it. Often the thinking is expressed in presentational vis-à-vis representational language. That is, "the music is 'cool'" or the music "blows me away." This is a distinction Wittgenstein

78

makes regarding a very different use of language. Representative language attempts to describe an event so as to make the language correspond to the object or event under examination. It is language as a "picture" of the world, in this case of music. In contrast presentational language is "an utterance" *(Ausserungen)*. An utterance presents one's state of mind; it doesn't represent it. To say that music is "cool" does not representatively describe it, but rather presents one's response to it.[12]

In popular culture, contemplation about music typically takes this presentational form. It is decidedly not contemplation in the sense of discursive explanation, description, and analysis; rather it reports impact, response, and these usually in metaphoric expression, for example, the music is "cool." Thus, it works with presentational expressions, and "contemplation" becomes something more like working with patterns of metaphoric utterance than with an analytic, explanatory, and representative discourse.[13]

In this sense "contemplation" is figural engagement in contrast to a more thoroughgoing semantic one. This figural engagement also has a definite sensate character to it. The figural claims about the music involve visual, auditory, rhythmic, luminous, movement, and danced, even explosive, expression. So music is not only "cool," but it "blows me away," it "gets to me."

To make this more concrete I talk with my eighteen-year-old grandson, Blake, this morning. He tells me that music that is "cool" can also be called "tight." I ask what this means. He says, "it means it's cool." So cool is also "tight." But music that is "cool" or "tight" can also be "bad" (meaning, of course, good). I ask what it means when you don't like music. He tells me it "sucks." His best friend here in Phoenix is another eighteen-year-old. When Blake's friend dislikes a song, he calls it "whack." If he likes a song, he calls it "gangsta," especially if it is rap. I ask Blake what these words mean. (I frame the question so that I am asking him for their semantic meaning though I do not use that word.) He answers: "I don't know; 'tight' just means you like it. 'Sucks' means you don't." "Gangsta" means it's good; "whack" means you don't like it. He also tells me that when he is going down the road and has the stereo playing loud, that this is called "blazing." He likes a heavy bass beat. I, of course, ask "Why?" "Because it makes 'you feel like you're in it.' It makes you feel like you are right there."

I cannot help noticing how figural and sensate his language tends to be. Words like *cool, tight, sucks, blazing,* and *whack* are certainly figural and sensate. Each time I ask for what they mean, I get either a slang synonym or I get a phrase indicating like or dislike. This is hardly the analytic or descriptive language of semantic discourse! Yet, I am in enough conversations with this generation to know how typical this language is, and my research in generational studies over the past twenty-five years suggests that this language use is quite typical of the largest modality in Blake's age group.

I do not mean to say that these expressions are entirely lacking in semantic meaning. But practices of literate discourse that attempt to make use of precise definition and carefully articulated claims, for instance, are not at the forefront of these practices. Neither do I mean to say that no one of Blake's generation engages this music in more typically contemplative ways. Some clearly do. Rather I am speaking to a modal range of practices that characterize a major response to music.

Let me be clear, too, that this does not mean we should ignore words in music. Even if words are not the focus or at the forefront of use, this does not mean they have no effect. Besides, in the church the words need to be intrinsic to the faith. This is an important corrective to the banality and just bad theology of a good deal of so-called "contemporary Christian music." Brian Wren, an important theologian and hymn writer, sees clearly the appropriate use of contemporary music, but he also knows that the lyrics are important and require critique. His is a sane and wise assessment of these issues.[14]

Yet, the response of the church must go beyond literate critique alone. Experiential engagement of the kind I address here is more aesthetic than it is semantically and analytically contemplative, but it has a decidedly "cognitive" character. That is, how the music sounds, its sonic impact, its percussive rhythms, and its referentiality relate pervasively to what younger generations regard as "real," "authentic," and "true." I think here of a contemplative experientiality in which the "real," the authentic, and the "true" are embodied, enacted, and performed. In settings like these the "contemplative" functions through contrast, juxtaposition, and fit rather than through analysis, representative description, or logical assessment.

For example, Radonna Bull of the Scottsdale Congregational United Church does a multimedia presentation which uses a hard driving rock song, "My Little Demon," in order to address one of the twelve steps in AA in which one has to admit that one is powerless to overcome one's addictions. In this piece she juxtaposes a host of images of things in which we are caught: alcohol and other drugs, sugar, unhealthy food, tobacco, narcissistic approaches to our bodies, and so forth. In the midst of these she places the text of Romans 7 with its statement of our caughtness, the ways in which we cannot do the good we would but do the very thing we would not. By using the juxtaposition of images, music, and Romans and by setting up jarring ways in which the biblical text names our compulsions, the piece embodies an experiential "critique" of our caughtness. In this piece the music provides the sonic "realness," "authenticity," and "truthfulness." In the church we need to understand that for most in the younger generations if worship does not sound right, it will not be true, it will not be genuine, and it will not be real. Music is intrinsic to this experiential "contemplation."

Music as Vision

Music as vision, as the statement of some ideal state of affairs or some sense of how the world is supposed to be is another important use. In this sense music enacts "ideal time." That is, it brings together many things not integrated in the ordinary time of our everyday lives. It can project states of life not realized in the everyday world. With its capacity to cross walls of hostility, with its expression of unities beyond our divisions, and with its projections of high satisfaction in the face of human yearning, music can enact a world where the impasses of the present with all their finitude, frustration, alienation, and contradiction are "healed" and "surpassed." In this sense music can "remember the future."

We see this in love songs all the time: that ideal woman or man who is the answer to all of one's dreams. The song then "describes" the life lived with such a person, with all the passion and resolution of the yearnings and hopes for a love of utter fulfillment and happiness. In that wonderful scene in Puccini's *La Boheme* where Mimi and Rodolfo meet, he sings "OH, sweet face suffused with the light of the rising moon, in you I see the dream incarnate I'd like to dream forever!"[15] Such expressions can be found across a host of genres. It is not the exception, but a common characteristic.

Still, it is not only in the love songs. The hope for a better world, dreams of peace with nature, reconciliation among the peoples of the world, songs of justice and freedom: all of these and more can be found in a host of genres of music.

One can argue that this kind of music doesn't mean much in terms of people's lives: that such love does not exist and those romantic love songs are quite distant from the actual relation-

82

ships of marriage and couples living together. Further, dreams of a new world are just so much "pie in the sky." They are an opiate or a kind of tipping of the hat by nice people who can acknowledge humane ideals that, nevertheless, don't have much to do with their lives. Mainly it serves status functions or escape-time amusement. Such claims characterize a good deal of the critique that is out there.

The use of music as enacting the future, however, takes on more gravity when it occurs in a community with an alternative story to that of the secular world. Further, when the use of music occurs in the church in a community with practices intrinsic to an alternative or oppositional story, a more formative process takes place. The point is that when music "enacts the future" in the storied community of faith whose practices serve that future, we have moved away from a commodified use of music for feel-good purposes. We have moved into an arena of ritualizing the future and of formation. This is no mere action of subjective choice to serve consumer demand. This is no longer a public of individuals joined largely around music alone, but a story-formed community engaging in practices that instantiate a different future in which music has a central place.

Furthermore, too much is made of knee-jerk, pie-in-the-sky charges. The uses of "remembering the future" serve a great many more functions than such critique usually recognizes. The ritual enactment of the future can be a heavy critique of the present. It can be a sharp challenge to the way things are. It can be a call to live a different reality. This is a radically different practice than that of "pie in the sky." In my study and research on the poor and on working people over the last thirty-five years I find this charge made against them by many who do not do the close descriptive work of how these practices are actually used. These charges often come from affluent "social critics" who are frustrated that the bottom half of the class structure won't enact *the critics'* views of the future.

It is silly to suggest that the church as storied community of faithful practice avoids consumerist practices or "pie-in-the-sky" escape. The church does not fulfill its story seamlessly. It often fails to be faithful. Still, the church at work in these alternatives is a different form of life and truly can shape lives in ways that both challenge the consumerist mode and offer another way to live in the world. In this faithful mission the use of music with its capacity to enact the future can be a faithful exercise of the church as alternative to the culture around it. We shall turn to these things later, but now we need to look at another dimension of music, that of rhythm and beat.

Music as Beat

The relationship of music to rhythm and beat is complex. I do not hope to capture exhaustively the uses of rhythm in music. My aim is decidedly more modest. I want to lay out some basic uses that relate to beat in contemporary music, which today have a special role in multisensory experience. That is, I want to examine a few uses that play an important role in the integration of image, sound, light, move, and dance and then to suggest briefly their implications for the church.

Sonic Logic

Simon Frith uses the concept of "sonic logic" in contrast to semantic logic to suggest the ways that meaning can be embedded in sound and percussion in contrast to their more exclusive use in language.[16] In this regard I find Wittgenstein's understanding of logic particularly helpful. For Wittgenstein "logic" has to do with "boundaries of proper use." I am using this characteristic in terms of sound, that is, how is sound, especially sound as rhythm and beat, properly used in a form of life? What boundaries govern its use?[17]

I am not looking for ahistorical uses of beat, but rather at conventions in a form of life, particularly in contemporary music, that convey meaning. While, again, this meaning is not without language, it is more presentational and more a practice of aesthetics and experience. That is, it has to do with getting the sound "right." It has to do with a certain "fit," with a kind of association of music with moods and feeling and with a group or community or public identity.

The best way to witness this "logic" is in its violation. For example, go to a party with people in their twenties. Then interrupt the music playing on the stereo with some genre quite alien to their aesthetics. If you are not met with revulsion and some kind of overt oral protest, you will find the twenty-somethings voting with their feet as they leave the room, or even the premises! Violations of sonic logic are not only instances of cognitive dissonance, but violations of "reality," of "authentic life," of "truth." It has the quality of environmental violation. Sonic logic is closely related to the distinction between "noise" and "music." I cannot help thinking here of the reaction of many younger people to easy listening music. It seems to me that the church is often playing "easy listening music," or the equivalent thereof, in worship.

Sonic Logic and the Experience of the Body

It is then but a short step to see violations of sonic logic in beat. In a previous book I reported on the change of beat in the wider culture of the United States from the generations born before World War II to the generations born after the war. Wilson Pickett's 1965 song "In the Midnight Hour" changed the dominant percussion of younger generations from the downbeat (emphasis on one and three) to the backbeat

85

(emphasis on two and four). Even today, when I am in a large auditorium I can still see the presence of different generations by the pattern of clapping. Those in the older generations clap on the downbeat, and those of the younger generations clap on the backbeat.[18]

Susan McClary points out the relationship between beat and the experience of the body. While she does not use the concept of sonic logic, nevertheless she observes that, when you change the beat of a people, you change the way they experience the body.[19] I contend that sonic logic is a basic aspect of the way we experience the body in contemporary music. Indeed, sonic logic and the experience of the body are internally related, meaning by that that you don't have one without the other. In this sense sonic logic is intrinsic to the paradigmatic sensibilities of sound. It is basic to the socio-cultural and historical constructions of who we are.

In the church we have given inadequate attention to this relationship of music and beat to the experience of the body by younger generations. If liturgy is the work of the people, it is very difficult to ignore this constitutive dimension of their lives. Furthermore, when the church associates only certain genres of music and certain kinds of rhythm and beat with the gospel, why is this not idolatry so conceived? Why is this not a cultural imperialism? Why is this not a violation of the missionary character of the church?

Sonic Logic, Differentiated Beat, and a New Sensibility

One of the challenges in the church today is that the generations have different sonic logics, and that these differences are growing, not only in degree, but also in kind. I have already mentioned the shift from downbeat to backbeat that occurred in the sixties, and its impact. We are now in an even greater change, I suspect, with the immensely growing popularity of

Latino/a music, especially its percussive and rhythmic power. For one thing, the complexity of beat is enormous. To move from, say, rumba to samba to meringue to salsa, to mambo to tumbao, to calypso to Afro-Cuban, and more (!) is sonically and rhythmically dismaying to one like me formed in a downbeat world. My paradigmatic sensibilities are not merely challenged. If I were to move rhythmically to such beats, I would "strip my gears" and "tear off my oil pan"![20]

But I have a granddaughter who is a different case altogether. She is "a special kid"; the technical diagnosis is that she is "developmentally delayed." One characteristic of her condition is that she is not well coordinated. While she skates in the Special Olympics, she still struggles with attuned physical action and with the body control necessary to perform at a high level either athletically or in other kinds of movement and gesture. Yet, she loves Latino/a music, and she amazes me with her ability to move with the beat and the gestures of the music. She has a physical frame much like my own. Her fingers and legs and walk resemble mine. I look at her and say to myself: "bone of my bone, flesh of my flesh." Yet, she is clearly encoded quite differently than I am. It is so very evident that she is *other*. More than that, with all of her disabilities she is so complexly "woven" in ways I do not understand and can only approach intellectually. When I attempt to "get inside" the sonic logic of her life and practices, I realize how much of an alien I am to her world.

The point is that a new sensibility is in formation in this culture. It comes, in part, from a new sonic logic and brings with it a new formation of the experience of the body. This sonic logic is increasingly a basic characteristic of multisensory and multimedia practices and experience. Its proper use connotes identity, authenticity, "reality," and "truth." This sonic logic, however, will be not only that of one new music and beat. We face the coming of a plethora of music and rhythmic patterns that characterize the larger population of this culture. Latino/a music will be only one of these new developments.

In terms of Christian witness the challenge of this differentiation of sonic logic is mind boggling. What this means for Christian witness is a challenge of the first order. At the least it means the development of new skills in the use of music in multimedia settings of Christian witness and worship. This means the church must learn to place this music in God's story. I think, for example, of the song "My Little Demon." I cannot now hear that song without placing it in the context of Romans 7.

In other cases this will mean the writing and generation of new music by the church, music that pitches tent with new musical forms. While this has begun on a large scale in contemporary Christian music, this music is very uneven in its faithfulness. We need the very best of our composers and musicians at work developing music intrinsic to the Christian faith and sensitive to the sonic logic of the culture. Finally, we need a vast experimentation by local congregations learning to do worship and witness faithful to God's story and embodying that story in these new forms of rhetoric.

In sum, I have attempted to look at basic uses of music in the United States today. While I have made no attempt to describe an exhaustive list, nevertheless five uses seem to be important. First, music is clearly soul music in the sense that people are encoded with it and that it tells the stories of millions of people in this society. As Ruth Finnegan suggests, it provides the most compelling stories of their lives. Second, it reflects and expresses feeling, and that across a great range of emotional life. Third, music serves as a ritual enactment of meaning. Its meaning is not something that stands behind the music and its practices, but is enacted in those practices. Fourth, while contemplation has an important role in the use of music in the past and today, "contemplation" with younger generations takes a more figural, sensate, and presentational form. It therefore poses a different kind of "thought," a practice to which we will return later. Finally, the use of music involves a sonic logic. While this logic is not confined to beat, I develop its use in this way to get at the ways it forms our sensibilities and the experience of our bodies. In all these uses I have attempted to show the implications of these uses for placing them in God's story.

These five uses of music play an important role in multisensory and multimedia experience. They are intimately related to the persuasive art of this experience. Music's encoding in our lives, its telling of our stories, its capacity to reflect and express feeling, its power to enact meaning and to form our being, its experiential "contemplation": all of these invoke/convoke wide ranging dimensions of our lives both individually and collectively. When combined with image, light, move and dance, especially as all of these are performed and not merely taken in, the power of persuasion takes on the character not of an external inducement but rather of a participative, enacted performance that calls forth the constitutive character of our lives. It reasonates with the constructed social, cultural, and historical nature of our very lives. When these are then placed in God's story—as our final aim and end, the ultimate source of all our desires, the lure of our completion—all these are engaged in the performance of faithful worship and witness, a practice that does not so much convince us of something outside us but poignantly "within" us and "around" us, both personally and corporately, but also awaiting us as who and whose we ultimately are.

But, I get ahead of myself. While the relationship these musical practices have to the uses of image, light, move, and dance are central to a better understanding of multisensory and multimedia rhetoric and its practice in Christian witness, we must turn to light and its role in this emergent complexity of the art of persuasion.

C h a p t e r   6

Let There Be Light

My friend Joel Ferrell works professionally in theater. His performance career includes roles as actor and dancer, and he now works as a choreographer and director. One day I ask him about the importance of lighting in the theater. He launches into ten minutes of the best material I know. A few things here can give a flavor of his comments. "In the theater I would rather have lights than scenery," he says. It is clear that for Joel lights can do much more than scenery. He also speaks of the role of light in bringing focus to the action on the stage and to its capacity to build intensity. At one point he says, "In the theater, if you have nothing going on, put a light on it!" This conversation leads me to further study and to a growing realization of how inadequately we address lighting in the church. That evening with Joel reminds me of sermons of my own where nothing is going on, and where light certainly might help!

The Power of Light

Hardly anything is more intimidating than to write a few paragraphs on light and its use. Basic to this intimidation is the history of light as seen both scientifically and spiritually. The wonderful book by Arthur Zajonc displays, on the one hand, the rich story of light as it has played out in the work of scientists like Galileo, Copernicus, Planck, Einstein, Hubble, and a host of others. On the other hand, he reviews the ways that the religions of the world understand the place of light in their relationship to God and/or ultimate issues.[1] My effort here is much more humble. What are basic uses of light today in contemporary practices like theater, concerts, stage productions, and other public events, and what can we appropriately learn from these for the worship of the church? Again, I can examine only a few such uses.

Lighting as the Glue

Richard Pilbrow is a world-class figure in lighting design whose book is arguably the best we have on stage lighting design. He names the integrative role of lighting, stating that lighting is "the glue" of a production. It "joins all elements of the production together and thus helps to underline for the audience the full emotion and meaning of the play."[2]

I think here of the capacity of light to serve the flow of worship, to move with the mood of the liturgy, and to indicate transition. It can prevent ruptures in the worship and enhance the focus, the ebb and flow of intensity, and the holistic character of the liturgy. What follows is an outline of a number of basic uses.

Intensity

Pilbrow names four properties of light that can be controlled and used in stage lighting. The first is intensity, the brightness of light. He points out that brightness is, in part, a function of our "subjective impressions." How a light appears can be more important than its wattage. A single lightbulb on a darkened stage can appear quite bright while a 1,000-watt light can seem dim in a highly illuminated setting.[3] Nevertheless, intensity is a function of changing light and the degree of its illumination.

I wonder here about church sanctuaries where the light hardly changes over the course of entire worship service. What is communicated at a subliminal level when the lighting of celebrative music about God's glory is the same as that which characterizes the confession?

Contrast also plays a powerful role in intensity. "The color and texture of scenery, costumes, properties and, indeed, the actors' faces also affect apparent brightness." Each of these effects, however, is different on a black-and-white stage setting. Yet, an audience adapts to light so that a brighter scene following a dim one may seem well illuminated but only for a short time. The intensity may need to be raised to counter this adaptive effect.[4] Again, there is an art to the use of contrast in worship. In my experience such things are not typically given serious attention.

Visual fatigue is also an issue in intensity. A dim scene can wear down an audience as can too much light over an extended time. Further, "rapid changes of intensity may prove tiring to the observer."[5] In these cases and others Richard Palmer observes that "A constant stimulus produces a diminishing response."[6]

In the church the issue is often not only fatigue, but boredom. Some services have a sameness that does not serve the liturgy and is hardly active praise and worship of God. No case is being made here for lighting as a panacea, but it is a resource. My suspicion is that many services can be transformed in their worshipful energy by a more faithful and artful use of light.

Visual perception, understood as the illumination needed to see stage objects clearly, varies in terms of color, the reflective capacity of an object, its size, and the distance of a spectator from the scene. The bigger the auditorium and the farther away the back rows the greater the illumination required.[7]

Some churches simply lack sufficient illumination. Careful examination of what is going on in a sanctuary in terms of lighting is a worthy study. What objects, for example, are central in the liturgy? What is the lighting? What events, actions need special illumination? Is the illumination commensurate with the importance of the liturgical moment?

The role of intensity in setting mood can hardly be overstated. For example, an audience is more attentive when the stage is highly illuminated and provides more of a capacity to see. "Bright light for comedy" is an old saw and tends to be widely applied in theater.[8]

In the church I think of the Christian year and of changes in lighting appropriate to the moods, for example, of Advent and Lent. Or, within a single worship service how does lighting serve the moves from gathering to proclamation and response and then to Eucharist and to sending forth? Or, how does lighting serve the shifts within each of these frameworks? In a culture where lighting is an indigenous practice in theater, in concerts, and in a host of settings of shared celebration, the church's attention to such matters is a basic form of pitching tent.

Sometimes more is not better in the use of light to build intensity. Pilbrow maintains that imaginative use is more important than simply more lights. He reports that in the 1970s the use of two to three hundred lights in a production was a great many, while today a thousand is not unusual. The trend seems to be toward more, not fewer, lights and with these a greater variety of lights with which to work. He states, "New light sources, giving new possibilities of powerful light with greater contrasts—deeper shadows—have arrived, and hopefully will allow stronger characterization of light, not just provide an ever brighter blaze of overall illumination."[9]

In the church we do know the power of the candle and its enormous capacities for setting mood and providing an illuminative context for worship and prayer. On many occasions it is just right. There are those times when anything more than candles is too much. At the same time, we may have too much confidence that the candle is enough. I remember a service that has seven candles as the only illumination for an hour and ten minutes. Such can, of course, be quite appropriate on some occasions. In that service, however, it is simply boring. In those settings I yearn for some illuminative texture to match the movement of the liturgy. I can think of a Tenebrae service where candles, virtually alone, might be quite appropriate. In a different service more lighting is needed to move through the different rhythms and flow of the liturgy so that moves from a song of praise to one of prayer or confession can indicate shifts of mood and pace and expressions of different forms of vitality and depth.

Color

Color on the stage is a function of the color of the light, the colors of the objects, and the impact of these on the eye. Color can provide emphasis and change or embellish the pigment in dress and background or other objects in a performance. New lighting technologies offer great freedom in uses of color, but Pilbrow argues that the basic purpose is "to enrich the visual and emotional atmosphere of the stage."[10]

Different colors serve different purposes. The yellow-green zones of the middle of the color spectrum help us see more clearly than those of the red and blue ends. Color also affects mood. Comedy uses warm colors and tints; tragedy works with cool or strong colors. Moreover, color is a powerful instrument for engaging the imagination.[11]

The light of the sun is mainly white, but the hour of the day, the weather, and the subsequent filtering of the atmosphere perpetually affect this. In contradistinction, Pilbrow warns that stage lighting "can be a sickly pinky soft mush." While the play determines the colors to be used, in times of doubt "cleanness and clarity" are the safest fallback.

Here, too, the church has much to learn. For example, what lighting serves best the dark wood furniture, altars, and backgrounds of many sanctuaries? Or, of those of a different color or makeup? Against these backgrounds what happens to the cross in its illumination or the communion table or the pulpit? What is the role of lighting in the display of the colors of vestments or robes or other dress? If a worship service is held in a room other than the sanctuary or a building other than a church, what consideration is given to the color and its illumination? These are not merely ornamental considerations but relate to the substance of liturgy and its rich sensory experience.

Distribution

The form and direction of light are the concerns of distribution. The right light from the right angle is central to good lighting. Pilbrow reports that the eye has a limited range of distinct vision, two to three degrees. Outside this limit our peripheral sight relies on "fairly crude stereoscopic vision." Exact focus on a face, for example, is key, and with that the drawing of attention to the point of interest in the performance. Pilbrow reminds us: "The eye is invariably attracted to the brightest object in the field of vision."[12] All these considerations make accuracy in lighting central to effective use.

I am sometimes in a church where the minister and other liturgists seem to meld into the background. You can see them, but they don't stand out. After a time, it becomes "work" just to keep focus; and unless the action or the sermon is good, your attention begins to waver. In my studies of light I learn that the theater uses side lights and top lights to prevent exactly this kind of melding of a performer into the background. A light at a forty-five degree angle from the front is not enough. I seldom see this kind of attention paid to lighting in the church. It is possible that some services are not so much boring as not appropriately lit. Some, of course, are inappropriately lit and boring!

Movement

The coming of moving light to the stage is a revolution in illumination. While it can overload our sensibilities, "Moving lights" offer "a new ability to alter light of three-dimensional character, filling stage space in real time in new and changing ways."[13] I want to add, too, that the use of moving lights opens a new opportunity for lights to imitate sound, especially in their rhythmic capacity. The percussive use of lighting provides new ways to integrate sound and the visual, a topic we shall explore in greater detail in later chapters.

We need to exercise care here. I do not want to suggest some tacky use of moving and beat-sensitive light in worship. I do not want a service to look like some twinkling saloon light or some make-do bursts of illumination. At the same time, moving and percussive light that coheres with and serves the liturgy and that embodies the mood and the flow of worship is an expressive form of response to God. To claim that this is not so entails an implication that the use of rhythm and movement in other sensory forms is also unfaithful. If this be so, is dance then ruled out in worship? Or, what happens to our auditory sense in the use of rhythm in music or the cadences and sometimes percussive use of words in preaching? To rule out illuminative rhythm, beat, and flow in worship is to excise an entire range of responses to God.

Five Aims of Stage Lighting

Pilbrow also examines the five objectives of stage lighting. The first is selective visibility. "The cardinal rule is: Each member of the audience must be able to see clearly and correctly those things that he [or she] is intended to see."[14] It is key that

97

audiences not have to strain to see. Such strain leads to weariness and then loss of attention, not to mention loss of dramatic effect in poor illumination. Under light, objects show up differently on stage. White objects appear brighter than dark ones, thus requiring specific illumination. Racial and ethnic skin coloring needs different lighting consideration. Action on a stage calls for a variety of uses of lighting: with some parts lit up, others in the dark, and with some actors more illuminated than others. Achieving balance in these settings is, of course, an important skill. The point of these considerations is to direct attention where it needs to be in the right light and to the right effect with color that provides the proper visibility.

In one sense this is the suggestion that people simply be able to see the liturgy. Yet, it is more than this. It is to see the liturgy rightly. It is to make prominent what is of central importance. It is to move the focus to the central act or event of the liturgy at any given point in the service. Further, it is to evoke the mood and the response appropriate to a liturgical act whether this is a celebrative song in praise or the shift to a pensive and explorative confession of sin before God.

The second objective of stage lighting is revelation of form. If objects are to be seen rightly in three-dimensions, shade and shadow become as important as light. This avoids a glaring distortion of form. In focusing on lighting, it is possible to ignore shadow and darkness. To focus on light to the neglect of shadow, however, is the same mistake as the focus on sound to the neglect of silence. Analogously, I think here of the role of negative space in the art of painting. Artists learn that negative space requires its own special attention. So it is with darkness and shadow.

These concerns are then key to liturgy. Imagine an evening service during Lent in which a life-sized cross is hung from the ceiling as the center of the congregation's attention. Then think through the role of light and the direction and shape of the shadow of the cross. The music then picks up the theme of cross and shadow to fit this occasion, perhaps the song "Beneath the Cross of Jesus" or some other. At this point the music is done in a slow and pensive way that calls forth the gravity and emotional engagement of Lent.

Composition is the third objective of stage lighting. The word "composition" is widely used in the painting arts. Pilbrow says that lighting is "painting the stage with light." "The intensity, color and distribution of light create compositions of light, shade and color over the setting and around the actors."[15] It also needs to be said that as important as a compelling visual stage is, it must not be achieved at the expense of what should be rightly and clearly seen.

By negative example, I think of church settings where altar, pulpit, and chancel are simply areas of a glaring sameness or dark monotony. Lighting offers a great diversity of compositions which fit the liturgical year, the different occasions and flows of the structure of worship, appropriate frames and settings for the preached word, and a way to lift up and display the centrality of the Eucharist. I appreciate the care and sensitivity many worship committees bring to the decoration and display of the altar. Lighting is a way of creating a wider composition of this kind of care and sensitivity.

Fourth is the creation of mood. Mood is in great part a consequence of selective visibility, revelation of form, and composition. Further, the emotional and psychological effects of light in a culture used in conjunction with these basic objectives provide the appropriate effect lighting design requires.

In lighting worship, then, mood is the artful and faithful result of the integrative and imaginative use of selective visibility, the disclosure of form, and "painting" the chancel, the altar, the sanctuary, and, most important, the liturgy.

Let me say here, too, that there is a movement in some churches to treat the congregation as an audience.

Consequently, the congregation is kept in the dark through a good deal of the service. I regard this as a major mistake. As I indicate below, the congregation is not an audience but a performing community of faith, enacting the liturgy. Lighting the community of faith, then, as the embodiment of the liturgy is central to the encompassing purpose of the service. To keep the congregation "in the dark" continually instructs them that they are an audience, not the central participants in the worship of God.

Finally, lighting conveys information. Pilbrow observes that in today's "speedier world" theater "tends often to speak in shorthand." That is, scenes "jump" from one to the next in contemporary drama. Lighting enhances this storytelling process by the ways it conveys changes in time and space. It grounds "the scene in its environment of the moment in the play."[16] The focus of Pilbrow's attention here is the place of lighting in the sudden shifts from one scene to another in much current theater.

Information is not an entirely adequate word for what Pilbrow addresses here, especially in the wider uses of light to inform the audience of what is coming. The context of his writing conveys more than some depleted notion of information taken alone. Several years ago at a Christmas Eve worship service, there was a very moving occasion in which each member of the congregation lit a candle in a completely darkened room while singing "Silent Night." It was a powerful and moving moment. As the song ended, however, the music moved abruptly to a different, upbeat rendition of "Amen! Amen!" the song made famous by Sidney Poitier in the film *Lilies of the Field*. It was a jarring rupture of mood and confronted the congregation with glaring white light. The sensitive tone and atmosphere of "Silent Night" seemed confronted with the glower of headlights. It took no little time for the congregation to recover and join in the wonderful lyrics of "Amen! Amen!"

Think what a difference a good transition could make here, especially in the use of light to close the one song and prepare for the next. Along with the music light can ready the congregation for the next song. The beautiful mood of "Silent Night" can conclude with the light holding that moment with the music. Then the music without breaking continuity modulates into "Amen! Amen!" but in a slow and pensive way while the lighting with the music builds in intensity and anticipation. The peace of that first Christmas night moves sensitively into a celebrative affirmation of its gift, "Amen! Amen!" What we then have is not a rude break from one song to the next but a transitional move from the experiential peace of that night's *gift* to a celebrative *yes* in response. In this move the light along with the music cues, informs, and constitutes the transition. It is in this sense that Pilbrow is suggesting the informational role of light.

In conclusion, the uses and aims of lighting design are foundational to the art. Yet, as foundational as these are, my outline of them is quite elementary. Even a brief perusal of the books by Pilbrow, Palmer, and others brings a sharp sense of the complexity of the field and the fact that it transcends technical expertise alone. It truly is an art, and in the hands of competent lighting designers an informed intuition seems to take into account these foundational uses and aims but then "takes off" in an intimate grasp that grows from long practice and skilled acuity in the field.

My research in lighting sharpens the sense of how inadequate the church's work is here. I recently spoke in a church that spent $125,000 dollars to "redo" the lighting in the sanctuary. I set up a computer, projector, and screen to lead a seminar that day only to discover that the bright lights of the sanctuary are directly on the screen. I asked them to turn those lights off. They told me that they cannot. All the lights are either "on" or "off." My suspicion is that the lighting architect "knew better," but just figured the church did not need anything more.

Similar stories with light occur again and again in my work with congregations. Very seldom do I find a church that thinks first of lighting the liturgy. Usually they light the sanctuary and perhaps the pulpit. Almost every guideline of lighting design is violated in the great majority of churches. We need a new sensitivity to the role of light in Christian worship and witness. I do realize that most churches cannot afford expensive lighting. The issue, however, is not how much one pays, but how thoughtful and imaginative and worshipful the use of light is. Further, to be clear, my point is not how we can work lights to manipulate people. It is how lighting can serve the integrity of worship, how lighting can serve the rhythm and flow of the liturgy, and how lighting can intrinsically serve to glorify and praise God.

Some years ago now, I lectured in class on the role of light, but apparently I was much too cautious in my claims. A student said to me: "Tex, you just don't get it, do you? You don't understand that in the twenty-first century electronic light will be as important in the church as the candle has been throughout the past two-thousand years." Perhaps this is an overstatement, but it is a word the church needs to hear.

It is difficult to exaggerate the role of light in multisensory rhetoric, especially when light functions in relation to image, sound, beat, movement, and dance. Before we turn to this synthesis, however, we turn first to the latter. The embodied character of movement and dance is basic to multisensory experience of a persuasive kind.

Chapter 7

Movement and Dance

The universe belongs to the dancers.[1]

Art and Dance as Illusion

My favorite dance performance of all time is Gene Kelly in *Singin' in the Rain* where he moves with such delight in a steady downpour. Every time I see it, I am caught up in the illusion of such celebration in a heavy rain. It is an illusion, and one in which I participate with relish. One can surely celebrate in a rainstorm, but that scene requires a certain illusory ambience to make it work. As much as I love it, I have never danced to an entire tune with musical accompaniment, a large camera crew, and a motion picture production company for backup while pelted by a heavy rain inside a large studio building, and I don't anticipate that I will. The scene works because of the illusion.[2]

Susanne Langer makes a great deal of the importance of illusion in art. She does not mean delusion or make-believe, but rather "disengagement from belief."[3] For example, when I watch Kelly dance in the rain, I disengage from the fact that I have never seen that happen in ordinary life. While it may occur, it is certainly not a part of most of our lives, I dare say, and certainly not with the staging and other appurtenances that accompany Kelly's wonderful performance. For Langer this illusion may resemble other things, but it consists entirely in its appearance. It is "a virtual object," an object "that consists entirely in its semblance, that apart from its appearance it has no cohesion and unity—like a rainbow, or a shadow."[4]

Illusion or virtuality is essential for art in Langer's work. The semblance or illusion of art "is its direct aesthetic quality."[5] In art this illusion is that of a "significant form," the essence of any art.[6] These significant forms are analogues of human feeling: hence her well-known definition of art as "the creation of forms symbolic of human feeling."[7] That is, Kelly's dance is an illusion, a virtual enactment of human feelings of delight, of celebration, of joy, and happiness. The lyrics exegete the dance:

> I'm singing in the rain, just singing in the rain.
> What a glorious feeling I'm happy again.

I wonder, however, what happens to dance when one moves from art to worship or witness. The embodied dance of worship and praise of God is actual, not virtual. It is not "disengagement from belief," but the enactment of conviction. It is not mere appearance, but concrete, material action intrinsic to the liturgy. In this sense, then, it is not art as Langer conceives it. It is worship. To be sure, it is art in the sense of the craft of dance. Though even here spontaneous dance in worship can be done by those not so trained and therefore not art in any highly skilled and developed sense.

There is an authenticity in the dance of worship not required by art in Langer's sense. Still, I think a distinction needs to be made between the virtuality of art in Langer's sense and the dedication of the artist to art per se even when engaged in a virtual rendering. The authenticity of art is, in part, the dedication to the craft and to the embodiment of the role or the feeling, or the virtual "reality" so enacted and danced. That is, when an artist engages in the performance of her or his art, the dance or the music may be virtual in terms of it representing a role or a passion; but *as an expression of art*, I dare say that most performers would not describe their artistry as virtual only. To put it briefly, the role or event performed may be virtual, but the art of doing so is not.[8]

In worship and witness, however, the danced action *is* the actual glorification and praise of God. I do not doubt, of course, that the subjective state of a dancer in worship can be other than one of worship and praise. It can be an "ego trip" or serve other aims extrinsic to the liturgy, but then, to that extent, it is not worship. In the same way dance as art can serve aims not intrinsic to the significant forms so engaged, but then it is not art in Langer's more complete sense. In saying this it is not my intent to diminish the art of a Gene Kelly. It is certainly not my intent to demean the art of dance. Rather, it is to suggest that something different is going on in dance as art and dance as worship and witness. I shall develop this in more detail as we move through this section.

Dance as Gesture and Imaginative Expression

Langer defines dance in terms of gesture and imaginative expression. She defines gesture as "vital movement," but vital movement as such is not art. Rather dance is gesture "motivated by the semblance of an expressive movement."[9] Only when vital movement is *imagined* so it can be performed does it become art.[10] Then it is a "possible dance-gesture." It is a "free symbolic form," one that can communicate "ideas of emotion, of awareness, and premonition, or may be combined with or incorporated in other virtual gestures, to express other physical and mental tensions."[11] In terms of the Gene Kelly performance it is not enough for him to make gestures in the rain, but rather these gestures must communicate the ecstasy, the transport of that "glorious feeling" of "I'm just singing in the rain."

Here, too, worship and witness are different. Dance as worship is surely gesture as vital movement; and when done in liturgical dance, dance attempts gesture motivated by expressive movement. Once again, in dance as art, semblance is central for Langer. In worship and witness, however, while semblance may be necessary for communicating through dance, in the enactment of liturgical integrity it is not enough. In art dance serves the craft and the virtual semblance of a significant form. Its authenticity resides there. In worship and praise dance serves God, its authenticity is in its intrinsic action of worship, praise, and witness.

Let me be clear here. I do not accept Langer's characterization of dance as its essence. I have no commitments to some ahistorical notions of what the essence of dance is. Rather, I am interested in Langer's characterization of a use of dance to distinguish the difference between dance as worship and dance as art. With respect to dance as worship and witness I see no narrow definition in search of some essence, but rather understand the uses of dance as intrinsic to the service of God. This leaves open a wide range of uses and is not limited to some one essence conceived in terms of semblance, virtuality, or some suspension of belief.

Dance as a Virtual Realm of Power

Langer argues that the prime illusion in dance is "a virtual realm of Power."[12] The movements of dance appear to arise from "powers beyond the performers." Langer points out that the relations between dancers in a performance are more than those in space alone. Rather the movements display forces at work invisibly. The dancers enact virtual energies that express will and agency, the conflictive and conjoining powers of attraction and repulsion, and the range of feelings that shapes and compels life.

Even in an individual performance like that of Gene Kelly's, we see this play of the forces of rain and embodied delight. In that memorable scene where he steps and stomps with one foot in the street and the other on the curb, he splashes his way through the puddles oblivious to the downpour. Actually, no, he is not oblivious; the drenching is essential to the enactment of the powers. It is the relation of dancer to the rain, among other things, that displays the energies of delight. It is the juxtaposition of rain that normally dampens our emotions that here becomes central to the display of the power of that "glorious feeling." Here we have no cry of complaint—"don't rain on my parade"—but rather a shout of celebration "I'm singing in the rain."

In dance as worship and witness there is clearly an appropriate display of the powers, but I want to argue with the word "virtual." In the church we deal not so much with the virtual as with the unseen. We worship and bear witness to the God in whom "we live and move and have our being," but we are addressed by and respond to the God we do not see. In the Eucharist we celebrate Christ whom we do not see. We are the church whose founding is in the Holy Spirit who is not available to our vision. Certainly there is a realm of power and powers to be danced in authenticate worship and witness, but these are not virtual. To be sure, our understanding, our grasp, our enactment of God's reality and glory are never adequate. Still, this is not a dance of virtuality; this is faithful gesture and liturgical expression in iconic enactment. The integrity of worship and witness lies not in its adequacy of the grasp of God but in its faithful enactment of God's story, in its attempt to point to God's work in the world and in the church.

The Transformative Use of Dance

I renege at Langer's characterization of all art as "the creation of forms symbolic of human feeling." I don't even know why we need one definition of art. Yet, I don't doubt that art is

used as an analogue of human feeling and that this is a significant use in our own time. Certainly this is an important role in
dance. But art and dance are so much more.

Francis Sparshott opens up another possible use of dance in
terms of its transformative power. He maintains that "Dance . . .
is a mode of behaviour in which people put themselves rhythmically into motion in a way that transforms their sense of their
own existence . . . that is at once characteristic and strongly
qualified according to the dance performed."[13]

This catches the formative power of dance with its capacity
to change us. I remember here Susan McClary's observation
about the relationship of rhythm and beat to the ways we know
our bodies. She claims, rightly, that when you change the
beat of a culture or a social group, you change the way they
experience their bodies. If this be true of rhythm and beat,
how much more is it so when these cadences are embodied in
movement and dance and these, too, as an ongoing part of
one's life.

I think here also of the importance of the hymnody to older
generations. Many have drawn their "theology" or their faith
claims and understandings from it. Clearly, music is formative
for their lives. In this connection Simon Frith notes that "dancing is to walking . . . as singing is to talking."[14] So I think how
much we miss in the church in the absence of dance as a formative practice. To be sure singing is a formative practice, and
an important one. It is also an embodied one, but the practice
not only of "walking the talk" but of "dancing the walk" takes
on new meaning and a new significance, and with it, of course,
of dancing and singing the talk.

Perhaps I have said enough already about dance serving the
integrity of worship and witness; but just to be clear, the practice of dance in these terms as formative and transformative is
central in the life of the church. In Protestantism in the United
States the church in too much of its history has focused far

more on getting belief right than it has on formation and being shaped by faithful practices. It is possible to spend most of one's time getting one's ideas or beliefs "correct," or developing one's point of view, but neglecting one's formation in the practices of faithfulness. I see dance, especially congregational dance, as an emergent and central practice for the church in the formation of our lives as a needed corrective to this too exclusive focus on beliefs and views.

Dance as Representation and Presentation

In our discussion of music above I use the distinction between representation and presentation. Certainly dance does attempt to do representation in the sense that by gesture, facial expression, posture, move, and so on it attempts to display or depict states of being, of human feeling, or of situations and conditions. These are more representational forms of communication. This is vital to its art. At the same time dance cannot be reduced to representative language about it. Representative language is inadequate to it. The American dancer, Isadora Duncan, says it well about the meaning of dance: "If I could *tell* you what I mean, there would be no point in dancing."[15]

A brief word is needed here about representation in worship as dance. One can argue that dancers even in worship may "re-present" significant forms not intrinsic to worship per se. For example, one can enact through danced signs forms of alienation, estrangement, and so on that are part of a worship service but not immediately in themselves worshipful. I expect such danced actions, however, to be dimensions of worship, else why be there? Still, in instances like these it is appropriate to speak of them as virtual in Langer's sense.

Still, dance goes beyond our attempts to describe what it is about in language. Judith Lynne Hanna, speaking from an anthropological perspective, reports that one cannot depend upon a native informant's descriptions of his or her own culture when it comes to dance. "The language of dance is non-verbal and not easily translatable lexically." Hanna observes that teaching and learning to dance in many cultures involves "dancing and watching, that is, without recourse to words." Lexicality does not encompass all our ways of knowing. Competencies take different forms, not the least of which are the move and dance competencies of the body.

Hanna reports that a good many of the characteristics of dance "lie beyond the conscious awareness of dancers and viewers." She points out that in U.S. culture most social dancers don't know the language for the specific moves and steps they make. Dance, moreover, has multilayered meanings, "Things taken for granted may not be articulated; lies, rationalizations, jokes, and metaphors are possibilities." Hanna compares dance to a Rorschach inkblot test. People project into it meanings that grow out of their individual experience and the conventions and interpretations of their more general cultural framework. While some cultures have codified systems and a rich nomenclature for different steps and moves and meanings, this seems not to be true of the vast participants of American popular culture.[16]

I draw from Hanna's observations the importance of the role of implicit knowing in dance. By implicit knowing I mean a kind of sensibility not articulated in representative language but nonetheless quite powerful in its capacity to shape the basic ways that people grasp life and the world about them when formed by ongoing practices—as one example— of dance. In terms of multisensory rhetoric dance is an embodied way in which one takes on a form of life at very basic levels of paradigmatic sensibilities. Dance participates in the very construction of our bodies and our understanding of "world."

My point here is that the enactment of dance as presentation goes beyond dance as representation. It expresses the praise and glorification of God that cannot be adequately represented in verbal signs alone. While it is not expressed without such signs, it can go beyond them. It can enact a "reality" that resides in the dance. In this way it not only represents, for example, ideas that "lie behind" the dance, but performs a reality that resides in it.

Dance as Alternative and Oppositional Practice

The formation of sensibilities in a form of life through multisensory practices like dance opens the door to the construction of alternative and oppositional communities. While dance can be a reflection of a society and an enactment of its basic beliefs and practices, it can also enact contrast and protest. It can, indeed, be a means of accommodation and of reinforcement of the status quo, but it can also challenge the powers that be.

Hanna illustrates this with the way dance was used by women in the 1929 "Women's War" in what was then called Eastern Nigeria. Women danced their grievances about taxation and abuse of the native representatives of the colonial government. When the British colonial powers refused to engage these grievances, it led to more violence and forced the powerful British to change their colonial administration.[17]

Dance emerges out of a form of life, but it also contributes to and helps to construct a "world." Dance can "frame" a message; that is, it can capture and place a message in context. In doing so it empowers that message. When the women of Eastern Nigeria place tax abuse in dance, it draws attention to and embodies the dynamics of such exploitation. To frame these abuses in sharply defined sonic movement and rhythmic gesture is a graphic display of the way things wrongly are, but it also calls for a "new world" and a counter "reality."

111

Congregational Dance

Let me underline at this point that my concern in this chapter is not only dance done by a few dancers "up front," but rather the performance of the congregation itself. I realize that this is rarely done in most denominations. Yet, dancing by the audience at a variety of venues is now common. I believe it has now become an indigenous practice at concerts and other performances in the culture. It is now even practiced at football games, a practice only done by the cheerleaders in my youth. So dancing by the crowd is not alien to the people of this culture. Mainly, it seems alien in church.

This is strange because dance is not absent in the Scripture. In the Hebrew Scriptures dance is performed in the worship of God (Psalm 149:3). Further, in 2 Samuel 6:14 David leads the Ark of the Covenant back to Jerusalem as he dances before the Lord. It may be a portent of things to come, however, that his spouse Michal finds it inappropriate; in fact, she despises him in her heart for his leaping and dancing (verse 16). Dance appears in a more negative light in the dance around the Golden Calf in Exodus (32:19). In the New Testament the appropriateness of dance is taken for granted when the Prodigal returns (Luke 15:25). While these are not many references, they are not radically prohibitive. Theologically speaking, I find it impossible to denounce dance as intrinsic worship and praise of God. While this does not condone abuses of dance, I do not see how it can be reduced to these abuses.

I realize, too, that congregational dance represents a host of skills we do not now have in the vast majority of churches. These skills will have to be learned. Some of these can be coordinated so that congregations learn movements and steps. This is done at St. Gregory's of Nyssa Episcopal Church in San Francisco and is done well. Such efforts as these, moreover, do not rule out more improvisational expressions. What we need, however, is a creative expanse of faithful experimentation.

Dance and Entertainment

When people object to dance and other figures of image, sound, beat, and light, the complaint is usually that they are being used as entertainment. It is clear from what I say throughout that entertainment is not under examination here. My concern is to worship and witness to God through the use of image, sound, beat, light, move, and dance. I make no case for entertainment in worship anywhere in this book, although I would not absolutely rule it out.

I must say, however, that I know this will not satisfy a certain group of more literately oriented people for whom a print-oriented service of worship is intrinsic to worship in their forms of life. It is not my intent to impose the forms of worship proposed here on those of a different cultural formation. The plain reality is that many churches provide more than one kind of worship service. It is not necessary for one of these to rule out the other. The problem more typically is for those committed to literate forms of worship to forbid those of a more multisensory and multimedia form. In such cases, I say, leave them to their uptight, self-inflated ways and let others get on with forms of liturgy that do indeed worship and praise God in a more fully embodied expression.

In summary and conclusion, a distinction between dance as art and dance as worship and witness is crucial. Dance as art may, indeed, use illusion to represent a range of human emotions, situations, and actions. Semblance and appearance are basic in such uses. Dance as worship and witness, however, is not appearance. It is a material and concrete practice of worship and witness. Here dance is intrinsic to worship. It does not so much seek to represent worship as to perform it. It is not semblance; it is the "real thing." It is not acting; it is enact-ment. Furthermore, dance as worship and witness does indeed, enact a realm of power. It performs the worship of and witness to God as the Creative, Redeeming, and Sustaining Power of the world. The powers of this God are not virtual, they are central to the conviction of the church. Invisible they are, but virtual they are not. Further yet, it is as the church engages in formative practices like dance that embody worship and witness that we are transformed and changed. Through such embodiment of worship and witness we become by God's grace the Body of Christ. The position taken here does not mean there is no role for representation, but representation is a dimension of a more intrinsic expression of worship and praise. Finally, dance can be an alternative and oppositional practice that not only resists the principalities and powers but offers the enactment of a contrast community.

We have come to the end of this brief description of the uses of image, sound, beat, light, move, and dance. Each of these brings special contributions to figural display, but they also share capacities to move and to form our very lives. The task now is to examine what happens when these are synthe-sized or integrated into a performative whole. As we shall see next, the "sum is greater than its individual parts."

Chapter 8

Figural Ensemble in Performance, Story, and Immersion

The integrative synthesis of image, sound, beat, light, move, and dance takes an event to a new level. It is a practice that offers more in its significance, its impact, than any one of these sensory experiences can provide taken alone. I call this practice *figural ensemble.* As I say, the whole is greater than the sum of its parts. The task of this chapter is to name what this "greater" is. I do this in two ways. The first is to name basic dynamics of the whole that move us to a new level. The second is to describe something of what this does in the performative, narrative, and immersive character of figural ensemble.

The Dynamics of Figural Ensemble

The first thing to say about the dynamics of figural ensemble is, obviously, that it is a far richer sensory experience. To engage an array of the senses on such scale is to raise the bar of participation. We not only see but hear. We not only hear but pulse to the rhythms of the occasion. We not only visually take in the scene but engage it in illuminative sweep, percussion, and ebb and flow. We not only move, but kinesthetically

115

enact the range of visual, sonic, rhythmic, and illuminative impact. Sensory range of this kind "takes off."

The second thing to note is the integration of these sensory experiences. It is not only that more of the senses are engaged but that they are synthesized and integrated in the event. As such a cohesion occurs, a unifying dynamic brings a crowd into full concert with the performance. This sense of collective and sensory unity generates bonding and identity.

A third dynamic is the way that the different senses themselves change when synthesized with others. One example, Walter Ong claims that "sound conveys meaning more powerfully and accurately than sight."[1] While I have enormous respect for Ong's work, this claim has an ahistorical cast and requires nuance in today's electronic culture.

Basic to his point is the way that sound "enters" us. It has a "special sensory key to interiority" in both a physical and psychological sense.[2] I am struck, however, by how much the visual now "imitates" sound in figural ensemble, especially in beat. The visual has become percussive and rhythmic in concerts and other venues. Lighting is now beat sensitive and accompanies the rhythm of the music and the flow of the performance. More than that, images are now keyed to the beat of the music and the lights, and each of these takes on an impact through assemblage that no one of them alone would have.

In Ong's terms, moreover, it is no longer possible to speak of sound as the only sense that enters us, even physically. Anyone who actively participates in a popular concert knows the powerful physical impact of image and light on the body. The brilliance of the lighting and the percussive character of the images and the lights make them more than an "external" experience. You can even close your eyes and yet not shut out the sensory impact of the images and the light. It is to be sure a different kind of "entering," but image and light do gain internal access to our inward experience. I find Ong's comment on sound too focused on sound as it works with an audience; it is not true of the crowd engaged in the multisensory and multimedia performance of figural ensemble.

The fourth dynamic is that figural ensemble is not only persuasive, it is formative. I argue throughout that rhetoric in its most powerful forms now occurs in multisensory and multimedia experience. Here, however, it must be noted how powerfully formative figural ensemble is. We address here not only persuasion but the very configuration of our lives in events of this magnitude and significance. Rhetoric can be thought of as an art that calls forth our assent; in figural ensemble the dynamic is not only persuasion but reconstruction. I do not, of course, maintain that a few of these can so shape our lives, but figural ensemble events of an ongoing kind clearly can.

Furthermore, such events can be very dangerous. Hitler may have instituted at Nuremberg the most powerful multisensory and multimedia events in modern history up to that time. Certainly there can be no question of the demonic capacities of events with this kind of power. At the same time, the church's birth at Pentecost is a multisensory event of great power. It even has an extraordinary "light show." So, central to these concerns is the question of which story is being enacted and what practices are called forth that are intrinsic to this story. In this sense the important question is whose story is being performed and what the character is of the event so engaged. For these reasons I turn in the remainder of this chapter to the issues of performance, story, and immersion. These not only disclose more of the dynamics of figural ensemble but provide additional clarity on the question of what or who is served intrinsically by such events.

Figural Ensemble in Performance

I have a videotape of Janis Joplin singing "It Ain't Fair" in the late sixties. It is a fine display of her artistic power and

117

capacity to wring emotion from a song.[3] Yet, what is so striking about the piece now is the percussion, the lighting, and the role of the audience.

In terms of the percussion, there is a drummer, but the visual display of the beat is done with the bass and guitar players hacking the air with their instruments and with Janis stamping her foot. Except for the drummer and, of course, the rhythm of the music and lyrics, that's it!

The lighting is constituted of standard forty-five-degree lights from the front along with side and top lights. There is also one gobo, which is basically a light that in this case turns slowly and shines on a wall behind the performers. It has some kind of stain on the lens to give it a psychedelic quality.

There may be an audience, but there is no indication of their presence. Except for Joplin and the band no one is there so far as one can tell. It may well be that apart from these few performers and the studio technicians working with them, they are alone.

In sharp contrast Tina Turner does a road tour in the late nineties, roughly thirty years later. She sings "Nut Bush," one of her signature songs. You are immediately struck by the percussive character of the event. Not only does the song have a backbeat, high energy rhythm, but the lights are attuned to the beat, and they flash, sweep, and move with it. Meanwhile, two big jumbotrons display images of the performance and enhance the sonic beat with visual cadence to match. Turner is not only backed by two drummers and a large band in physical movement as well as musical concert with the beat, but is supported by three singers who sing and dance in physical, sonic, and percussive accompaniment to Turner's magnificent artistry. Beat is everywhere in the performance: in sound, in image, in light, in move, and in dance. In this setting rhythm and beat are ecological.

There must be hundreds of lights at work in the performance. Shining down are not only those that sustain a bright luminosity for the band and the other performers, but dozens of others that sweep the stage and the audience and yet others that flash to the beat of the music. Here lighting is not only the glue, it is the visual "atmosphere" of the performance in which the event "lives and moves and has its being."

Turner is on stage in front of what looks like a crowd of about twenty to thirty thousand people. But this is no "audience." This crowd, rather, is actively singing and dancing and, I say, *performing* with Turner in the event. During the song she climbs down from the stage onto a lower level about waist-high to her fans. At this point she begins a call and response with the crowd. She sings-shouts "One more time!" and they respond with a roaring "Nut Bush!" Again and again she continues this interactive performance with them while she and they sing, dance, and shout. This is no passive audience here merely to see and hear Turner. This is a tribal gathering here to perform the show with her.

Audience as Performer

I know of no better illustration of how much performance has changed in the last thirty years. I certainly mean no slight of Janis Joplin in this comparison, but rather to point out how the practices of such events have changed. Today performance is not merely something done by the artist in the presence of an audience. Rather the artist and the audience perform it together.

Another example occurs in the warm-up act's increasing responsibility for getting the audience "into" the performing role. I remember a concert when Cyndi Lauper works as the warm-up for a Tina Turner concert. As she moves into her performance, it is clear that she is not getting the fully engaged response she desires. She runs down off the stage and heads straight for the first rows of the crowd and dives headlong into the people. When they catch her and "surf" her back to her feet, the audience roars in participative tribute. From then on the crowd does not merely look and listen, they perform with Lauper and later with Turner.

This performative role for the audience is now basic. In this role one should not miss the place of the figurative forms of multisensory and multimedia experience. Garth Brooks uses very effectively a highly focused spotlight to isolate two or three people in the crowd and then to display their picture on the full jumbotron screen. Or, a sweeping image of the entire crowd is often flashed across a screen to the participative delight of those gathered. And, of course, there are the bigger-than-life images of singers and musicians on the huge screens to engross more fully and involve the crowd.

Along with the images are the soul musics of people there gathered, which they associate with the artists. So the audience often sings with the artist and "rehearses" their own stories while giving expression to the encoded meanings of the songs in their bodies and lives.

Further, to love the work of an artist is to be formed in some way with the sonic logic of his or her work. As the visual, sonic beat sweeps "through" and moves "into" a crowd, the rhythm becomes collective, not only sung but also now clapped or swayed to, or danced or captured in other gesture and move.

In these venues light is the glue Pilbrow speaks of. The light not only accentuates the rhythmic, percussion of the fast-paced song but also slows down the event with changes of color or speed of movement in a tune with a different touch. The high energy of an upbeat piece transitions to the slow pace and altered mood of a pensive ballad. The lighting coheres with these changes of mood, indeed, often initiates the shift. And the audience-as-performer "on cue" responds and acts under the direction of the light.

At the same time, the audience moves and dances with the images, the music, the beat, and the light. Their involvement is not that of passive, sit-still listeners, but of active, dancing performers. While they do not share the stage, they do nevertheless fill the event; and they do so as a moving embodiment of this multisensory, holistic experience. This is the form that concerts and spectacles increasingly take in this culture. These are now indigenous practices. They are, at least, among the most powerful practices of bonding and commitment at work in our society today. They are at the peak of the formats that rhetoric now takes in its most persuasive forms.

So, the first thing to say about figural ensemble is the way that image, sound, beat, light, move, and dance work together to construct an audience as performer where each of these figural experiences work together not only to intensify the full sensory magnitude of the event but where the strengths of each of the figures feeds those of the others.

Implications for Worship

The implications for the church are profound and far-reaching. I think of typical worship services where people mostly sit and where the premium is largely on listening to talking heads. Even when we speak of "more participation" in worship, it is much too little. Performance is far more than mere participation. Participation sounds too much like "something is going on and I am going to involve myself in it." As I use the word, performance carries the sense that one is intrinsic to and organically constitutive of the event. It is not so much something we join, but something we activate, something that does not happen unless the body, the community does it.

Let it be clear, by performance I do not mean entertainment. I mean performance in the sense of taking something through to its aim or end, or to complete or finish it. My point is not how we can do something to amuse people, but rather how we engage people as performers of worship, and how we do so in multisensory and multimedia environments so that the liturgy is taken through to its aims, so that praise and thanksgiving are enacted as response to God.

Performance is not only a "receiving" of the gospel, it is an enactment of that reception. Meaning is not only communicated but embodied. It is not only thought but incarnated. It is not merely a subjective experience individualistically appropriated but communal action carried by the people of God in response to the Divine Gifts of Creation, Redemption, and Empowering Presence. In multisensory and multimedia practices it is to love God with heart, soul, mind, and strength in image, sound, beat, light, move, and dance.

Story

We see above the importance of story in providing context for images and for its role in soul music as the telling of one's story. In sonic logic, especially beat, story gains authenticity, and "truth" through rhythm and percussion. If one does not make the right sound and beat, the story will not be authentic, "true," or "real."

Again, lighting, as the glue, has the capacity to work with plot and with the ebb and flow of intensity. Lighting uses color to follow the shifts of the story. It distributes light to illumine that story and to achieve the narrative composition necessary to "paint" the liturgy. It brings resources to focus action and intent and to reveal the three-dimensional world of the enacted drama or concert. These are but a few of the ways lighting not only augments but also "tells" the story.

As we see above Susanne Langer characterizes dance as art as "a field of virtual powers" in which implicitly "there is always the recognition of created dance forces, impersonal agencies, and especially of controlled, rhythmicized, formally conceived gesture begetting the illusion of emotions and wills in conflict."[4] In dance as worship and witness I maintain that we are addressed not by virtual powers, but rather by the invisible but real powers of a Triune God. In dance as worship and witness the relation of God's story to dance is clear. Its display of God's powers, its capacity to present human action and will, and to display human bondage and spontaneity bespeak its narrative power. Even more, dance does presentationally what story in word can never fully achieve. It embodies and enacts what cannot be adequately said but must be shown and done.

To attempt to pull all of this together, figural ensemble constructs story in a more fully orbed way. Images, especially in their referentiality, call forth a range of experience and play across our memories. They call forth our own stories and provide opportunities for these narratives to be placed in larger, more encompassing ones. Soul music more directly tells our story and brings an encoded pattern to figural ensemble. Sonic logic provides an authenticity and "reality" to this synthesis. Light provides not only glue but a directing, focusing, moving, and transitional atmosphere to these moments. And dance becomes an embodied vortex in which all of the senses are employed in the performative work of enactment. These few comments, of course, do not exhaust the dynamics of figural ensemble in story, but rather suggest something of their integrated impact.

It is difficult to exaggerate the importance of story. I think of Hauerwas's point that stories operate through us. These stories are often not fully conscious to us, but we are always already governed by stories that shape our very lives, the ways we think, the structure of our feelings, the formation of our desire, and the commitments and aims we serve. Today the church faces a world where extraordinarily powerful practices enact and embody the stories of consumer capitalism and the self-interests of the nation state. If the church is to be a counter story, if it is to be an oppositional story in an electronic and digital world, it needs to pitch tent with indigenous practices like those of figural ensemble, but to do so with an alternative narrative to that of the powers and principalities. To do so requires that the practices of multisensory and multimedia rhetoric intrinsically serve God's story and not the other way around.

The Immersive Character of Figural Ensemble

In my junior year of college Peter Bertocci, the Borden Parker Bowne professor of philosophy at Boston University, came to my school, Millsaps College, for a lecture series. In his first evening presentation he spoke two hours and fifteen minutes, usually enough to wear out any audience. But I do not remember even breathing. I was riveted to his every word.

Bertocci's voice sounds like a barrel of nails falling down a heating and cooling duct. It is a gravelly, scratchy sound; but he generates great power with it. The very character of his voice seems to add authenticity and realism to his lecture. Till that time no speaker ever so captivates my attention, and I am not alone in that fully attentive crowd.

I now characterize such events as absorptive practices, and I associate them particularly, but not only, with literate culture. In this section on the impact of figural ensemble, I sharply contrast such absorptive practices with those of an immersive kind. I associate the latter with figural ensemble and with electronic and digital culture. I certainly do not wish in any way to disparage the extraordinary work of Bertocci in that series. It changed my life. Such events even today can speak profoundly to people whose sensibilities are formed by literate practices of an absorbing kind. Still, I contend that the practice of immersion is of a different order than the practice of absorption, and that immersion is the more powerful practice of rhetoric today and the one increasingly more indigenous.

The root word for *absorb* is the Latin *absorbere* with *ab* meaning *from* and *sorbere* meaning to drink in, to swallow up, or engulf completely. Synonyms for *absorb* are consume, engulf, imbibe, drink in, suck up, engross. In contrast the word *immerse* comes from the Latin *immergere*. The root of *im* meaning in or into and *mergere* meaning to dip or to plunge.[5] So the practice of absorption is one of "taking in" while the practice of immersion is one of "entering into," "to plunge into," "to dip into."

These distinctions are critical in describing the differences in the practices I have in mind here. Think of print as involving distance. We hold the book, the page, *away* from us. To be fully engaged with a book is to take it in. Visually we take it in. This is what I did with Bertocci's lectures, only in a combination of seeing and hearing.

This is a basic practice for me. My grandson, Blake, is quite different. He buys a CD player and a *surround sound* audio system. I ask why he needs six speakers. "Oh, Grandpa, so you can be in it. You feel like you are just in the music." In contrast, at our house the *stereo* set is in one corner of the room. We listen to it "over there." We "take in" the music, but Blake "swims" or "bathes" in it. Listening to him, I realize that I am still more into absorption than into immersion, though I do, at least in part of my life, engage practices of immersion in settings of figural ensemble. At the same time I am struck by the difference in the sensibilities of Blake and myself. A major shift has occurred.[6]

In a 1998 article B. Joseph Pine II and James H. Gilmore contend that the economy has entered a new era. No longer are we in a goods and service economy but rather in an emerging experience economy where businesses do not primarily sell commodities or services but rather experiences. For example, a consumer goes to a store for the experience of being there and may well pay for the experience. In most cases, they will go for the experience and buy something as part of their engagement with that setting.[7]

Pine and Gilmore describe such experience as made of four "realms of experience" which compose "spectra of . . . two dimensions." An experience can be active or passive, and it can be absorptive or immersive. These four dimensions are then imaged this way:[8]

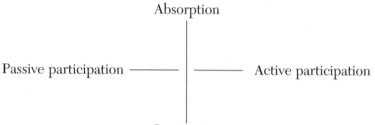

Where these four dimensions cross, say Pine and Gilmore, they form "a sweet spot" in which "the richest experiences . . . encompass aspects of all four realms." I find myself at odds with this graphic formulation. I do not doubt that "passive" and "absorptive" dimensions participate in events I describe as performative and immersive, but the very character of these latter practices changes the former. Hence to describe them as "passive" and "absorptive" distorts their concrete, material character. In figural ensemble what occurs is more like a "giving" and a "receiving." Neither the "giving" nor the "receiving" is passive. And in performative action there is, of course, focus and attention. There is a "taking in," but it is of a very different kind. It is the difference between seeing and hearing the action and being "in it."

Pine and Gilmore take this formulation in a consumer direction. They describe the process for "designing memorable experiences." "Five key experience-design principles" are named and developed: first, "theme the experience"; second, "harmonize impressions with positive cues"; third, "eliminate negative cues"; fourth, "mix in memorabilia"; and fifth, "engage all five senses."[9] This is a self-conscious, consumerist approach. It is clearly a grossly accommodationist stance. It seeks to find what experience people want and then attempts to provide it. Clearly, they are selling.

The church is not in the selling business. To be sure, there are churches that clearly sell out to the consumerist model, but the faithful church is not dealing in commodities but in Gift. We imperil our witness and distort the mission of the church when we buy into the consumerist form of life. I separate sharply an intrinsic use of figural ensemble to express the story of God in performative and immersive practices from that of a utilitarian use of such practices to sell commodities.

Furthermore, I am struck by the ways in which Pine and Gilmore "design experience" so that all the cues are "positive" and all the "negative cues" are eliminated. Where is the critical component in this position? For the church, where is the prophetic dimension of its life? My problem with so much of the use of multisensory and multimedia worship is the absence of critique. It too becomes pathetically accommodationist.

My point here is not now to find a way to insert the critical distance of the print world into figural ensemble and immersive events. Rather I argue that while we do need critique—and we continue to need critical distance—we also need critique of a different kind. The practice of critique in figural ensemble is not the critical *distance* of the literate world, but instead is the critical *immersion* of electronic and digital culture. This is a practice we will address in considerable detail below.

In sum and conclusion, in previous chapters we examine the ways in which the figures of image, sound, beat, light, move, and dance are used in contemporary forms of life. In this chapter I argue that the integrated synthesis of these figures is more than what any one of them does alone. The holistic impact is greater than the sum of its "parts." I demonstrate this not only by describing the interactive impact of these figures on each other, but also by examining what happens in the use of figural ensemble in performance, in their uses to "tell" a story, and in the practice of immersion. I am also actively intent that such usage be intrinsic to the worship and witness of the church.

We are ready now to turn to their more explicit use in the formative and prophetic life of the church, first in the prophetic use of figure and then in the use of critical immersion. We turn to the former in the next two chapters and to critical immersion in chapter 11.

Part Three

The Prophetic Church in Electronic Culture

Chapter 9

The Prophetic Use of Figure in Hebrew Poetry

One of the basic questions about electronic culture and the use of figural ensemble is its capacity for critique and for prophetic challenge to consumer capitalism and idolatrous patriotism. Both of these are major challenges to the church. Indeed, among the church's most dangerous accommodations are its collaboration with the metaphor of marketing and its collapse of Christian faith into an inordinate love of country.

For example, central to the dangers of consumerist capitalism is its capacity to turn every thing into a commodity. Notice how often one hears the comment in the church that "After all, we are in the selling game, and we are here selling the gospel." Implicit in such a statement is that now the Christian faith is simply one more commodity to be sold. What happens to the church's central claim that the good news of Christ—in the creation, redemption, and fulfillment of history and nature—comes as the gift of a loving and merciful God?

In addition, how does the church make a distinction between an appropriate love of country and complicity in nationalism, in which the nation state becomes an idol? The image that comes to my mind is the Sunday nearest the Fourth of July when the Crystal Cathedral drops an American flag across the entire front of the sanctuary. This "liturgical act" completely obscures the distinctively Christian symbols in the room and overwhelms the entire service with the central symbol of the American nation state. It is an idolatrous practice.

The issue of idolatrous patriotism is an even greater problem in the United States than perhaps ever before because of the power we now have in the world. There is no nation that can check the power of the United States. Furthermore, no nation has the capacity to advance the defense of its own interests as the United States does given its mammoth media resources. It is arguable that this country is more dangerous today to the people of the world than any time in the past.

To pitch tent in an electronic culture requires serious attention to these questions. How do we approach the issues of prophetic ministry? Can figural ensembles of image, sound, beat, light, move, and dance be anything more than complicity with the powers of the world? Can a church that pitches tent with these practices take on and call into question the atmospheric character of the ethos that surrounds consumer capitalism and the nation state?

A second question follows immediately upon this one. It is the question of formation. What does Christian formation look like in an electronic culture? It is crucial for the church not only to engage the practices of a culture but also to be an alternative community that enacts practices that are distinctively its own.

Hebrew Prophecy, Kings and God

To begin an answer to these questions, I want to look back into our tradition and its roots in ancient Israel. We can learn from Hebrew poetry practices that address issues that challenge us in our own time. I find especially helpful here the work of John Milbank. To be candid, I take Milbank's work in a direction he does not go. I see myself applying his work, and I hope faithfully so.

Milbank addresses the difference between pagan and Hebraic uses of language, especially the latter's use of language in poetry.[1] His concern is the use of language in ways that are not deceptive, that is, that do not serve the dominant power of a society. For example, in pagan religion divine language was used coterminously with the names of royalty. That is, the pharaoh was described by and named with divine titles. Milbank is interested in the ways that Hebrew poetry kept a tension between the use of words about kings and language about God.

Nations and Buckets

Using the work of Robert Lowth in the eighteenth century, Milbank characterizes a dynamic in Hebraic poetry as "diachronic figuration," that is, the use of figures across history. The chapter in which Milbank lays out his view is more than a little complex. For my purposes here I can describe this dynamic in terms of certain key characteristics.

First, Milbank points out *the wide use and highly repetitive character of figure* in Hebraic poetry. This use involves *"a repetition with variety."*[2] For example, the use of wilderness is a constantly recurring figure in Hebrew poetry. It appears in the Exodus, of course, as the Hebrew people wander for forty years in the Sinai. Yet, in Isaiah 40:3 the wilderness metaphor is used again, only this time as the place where the way of the Lord shall be prepared, a place that shall be made straight—no little achievement in the wilderness. It will be a highway for our God. The point is the figure of wilderness appears and reappears in the historical struggles of Israel whether in the time of Exodus, or the eighth-century prophets with the threat of Assyria, or in the sixth century with the struggles against Babylon, and so on.

Milbank describes how this kind of repetition *not only supplements but expands the meaning of God's work* with the prophets and the people of ancient Israel. These repetitive metaphors and figures relate the faith to a great expanse of places of nature (mountains, valleys, rivers, and wilderness), on the one hand, but also display the range of God's relationship with the Hebrew people in history, on the other.

Second, *these images are used metaphorically and remain figurative*. They take on a constancy, but "not a literal one."[3] The images are "simple and direct" and have "pointed effect." They take on a "fascinating obscurity," meaning that they invoke "a concrete yet general picture" that can be read many ways. The result is a "heightened poeticality." Yet, it is a heightened poeticality with prophetic effect.

I think here of Isaiah's language that before God "even the nations are like a drop from a bucket, and are accounted as dust on the scales" (40:15). When you think of that phrase literally, it is a strange one, an obscure one. How on earth can a nation be like a drop from a bucket? Yet, it is a very concrete picture. Somehow, it relates to the ultimate insignificance of the most powerful entities in the world. The testimony of Isaiah is that nations are like a drop or like dust on a scale. Can one really do more to relativize the nations than that!

Third and quite apparently, *these figures are about commonplaces (topoi)*. The figures are of wilderness, rivers, mountains, valleys, plains, shepherds, bread, wine, cities, people, nations, and all the rest. They come from "common life, from the most general and habitual circumstances of a primitive *agricultural* existence." Milbank quotes Lowth that the Hebrew language was "not remote from the senses."[4]

Further, these figures and the metaphorical applications of them are used over and over again. As a result they become a very *"concrete classification."* As such this daring but ongoing practice of reference takes on in everyday use a tremendous reservoir of meaning.[5] For example, the river Jordan takes on rich reference not only as an entrance to the land of promise but as the place where we cross over into death, among other uses.

Fourth, Milbank argues that in such poetry *"the perception of the environment and projection of value" arise together*. The result is that this "common stock of natural phenomena" become very significant in that they are made up of things quite common (for example, growth and decay) but also take on meaning and value of an unusual and extraordinary kind (like the flood and the exodus). *These commonplaces become the central reference point by which the Hebrews understand their lives*. Further, these concrete commonplaces provide an unending application that is open-ended even while it is tied to the particular history of the Hebrew people. To put it too simply, *the things of everyday life and the events of their history become loaded with significance, and the images and figures of the Hebraic faith tradition inhabit the world of the ordinary and the extraordinary*.

Fifth, Milbank points to a *"double play between two poles."* One is the Hebrew inclination for "the imagery of nature," for natural powers and works, and the other "can equally stand for the divine or human spirit." In the play of such poles Milbank, following Lowth, finds a *"reciprocal echo."*[6] In other words it is a back and forth echo where each plays off the other so as to enrich and supplement the other. The natural pole has an ambiguity that allows for a wide diversity of application, yet in its concrete expression does not lack clarity of meaning.

Think here of the image of a mighty rock. Anyone who knows desert heat and the shadow of a large rock or a mountain understands what a respite it can be. It is no stretch of imagination to see the powers and works of such natural imagery. When this kind of imagery stands for the enduring faithfulness of God, it takes on a great range of meanings that are infused and pervasive in and through life. For example, the God to whom we cleave in amputational grief, the One to whom we go in abject and unrelieved failure, the Balm of healing in the face of terminal illness, the Rock who is our salvation, the granite support of a people oppressed: these are among the vast range of uses such natural imagery can take when applied to human life before God. Here we see the power of the polarities of natural imagery and of human pathos and hope placed before God. Neither of these poles is more "literal" than the other, but each "rises finally to the tension between divine and human."[7]

Moreover, this reciprocal echo stands on no ground of knowing. *This ungrounded meaning gives it an obscurity that makes it all the more available across an inexhaustible range of pain and healing, of defeat and hope, of despair and conviction.* Until one does, indeed, throw oneself upon such trust in God, metaphorically, and figuratively does engage God as the Rock of one's life, how *can* such things be understood? In such practices we find a Strength otherwise not known.

But I do not mean only to individualize this point. *This dynamic is the language and faithful construction of a tradition, of a people* living through time who come to know who they are and how they can continue to live because the form of their lives is based not in a knowing but in the One who finds us in metaphor and figure, who can be trusted in spite of all "empirical" evidence to the contrary.

As this reciprocal echo between natural images and divine/human relationships is stretched out across time, *such poetry turns into prophecy.* By prophetic in this context Milbank means that the reciprocal echo involves not only clarification but supplementation over time, an adding on to the tradition.[8] Hence the tradition grows in its critical understanding of kings and its relativization of the powers of the nation. It displays the vulnerabilities of idols as a finite parading as infinite claims.

Milbank observes that this repetition-with-variation tradition is basically *oral, not written.* For this very reason it links the necessary repetition of ideas in words to the "prophetic" unfolding of always incompletely grasped [commonplaces] in time, through a series of performed human utterances. In other words, this reciprocal echo *achieves its height of expression in oral performance.* Milbank also claims that a rhetoric which operates through a repetition with variety "(which to be valid must involve an 'amplifying,' non-identical repetition) is peculiar to a biblical construal of reality and so implicitly, to its "ontology," its understanding of the way things are before God.

Sixth, Milbank makes a good deal here of *how important it is for the images and other metaphors to be embodied in events with certain concrete expression of what they convey.*[9] Here I read Milbank to say that if such utterance is not embedded in the practices of a living community, a tradition, it is dead. If, indeed, it is "merely" [my term] pure writing, it is nothing.[10] This underlines the performative role of a community in the context of a living tradition. That is, the performative work of a community engaged in the ongoing use of figure is intrinsic to its living out a story. Such performance provides the material practice for this interpretive action and self-understanding. To put it more graphically, a public, taken alone, cannot carry this performance. It requires a community. Individualized or socially disembodied spirituality cannot bear the Gift of such interpretive memory and hope.

Finally, Milbank supports Lowth's point that the repetition in Hebraic poetry is not so much a result of the paucity of the resources of their language but rather an indication of *the copious character of their images* and *the abundance of the commonplaces of their existence.* The Hebrew prophets have much to draw on in terms of figure and commonplace.

This results in communicating the same idea in a host of different ways. Such communication is "oral," in that it has the copious character of oral communication. With this a vast number of "synonymous signs" become embedded in the very practices of understanding and in addressing the variety and

137

change of life itself, indeed of history. Such communication is wedded to "spoken" performance.[11]

Such signs clarify, they do not foreclose. They add on; they do not merely defer meaning or abstract it beyond the grasp of a community but rather operate, as words that are employed, in the crunch of being embedded in the concrete life of a living tradition. In this sense the copious use of repetitious commonplace figures with variety across time opens the tradition and the community to the ongoing account of God's work in their midst. Moreover, the reciprocal echo of "natural" imagery and significant cultural events "sound off" in relationship to the divine/human story striking fire in the imaginations and the convictions of a people of the story.

For example, when Jeremiah (10:5) can say that "your idols are like scarecrows in a cucumber field," and Isaiah can cast the nations as a "drop from the bucket" (40:15*a*). Or when Ezekiel can say:

> All the trees of the field shall know
>   that I am the LORD.
> I bring low the high tree,
>   I make high the low tree;
> I dry up the green tree
>   and make the dry tree flourish.
> I the LORD have spoken;
>   I will accomplish it. (17:24)

Or listen to Habakkuk:

> What use is an idol
>   once its maker has shaped it—
>   a cast image, a teacher of lies?
> For its maker trusts in what has been made,
>   though the product is only an idol that cannot speak!
> Alas for you who say to the wood, "Wake up!"

> to silent stone, "Rouse yourself!"
> Can it teach?
> See, it is gold and silver plated,
> and there is no breath in it at all. (2:18-19)

In prophetic poetry and writing like this, *the very things and places of common life become central to the tradition of faith.* In such writing the natural world, the wood and metal of common existence, the operational day-to-day tasks, things like fields and cucumbers and scarecrows, and the juxtaposition of buckets and nations, suddenly become the metaphors with which one attempts to understand and practice devotion to God. But it is more than that. These prophetic uses of figure transform the very sensibilities by which we engage the world as a community of faith.

Yet, it is not only that one continues to arrive at new ways to see God's work but also that *nature and culture become filled with images of the workings of God active in history and in common life.* The polarities of these figures, on the one hand, and that of the God of history, on the other, become complementary. As "echoes" they reverberate, they jangle the world with a God who will not leave us alone, who speaks to us out of wind and fire, sound and fury, gold and silver, trees and grass, earth and sky, and sun and moon. This God acts in the midst of slavery and in the faithless idolatry of life in the promised land. And when all is lost, this same God remembers teaching Ephraim to walk and says to the same sinful and wayward people that indeed they shall receive comfort and that their warfare is ended.

Milbank's work on the role of figure in Hebrew poetry has rich implications for the use of figure in electronic culture and contemporary life. Its use of figure across time, its communication through the commonplaces of ancient Israel, its construction of everyday life as loaded with significance, and its capacity to form echoes between the things of lived existence and the activity of God in the world resonate with implications for our own time. We now live in a world of enormous commonplaces but of a different kind. While we certainly have rivers, mountains, valleys, and the rest, so much of of our common life is filled with images, music, beat, light, movement, and dance. More than that, the pervasive presence of popular culture and its increasing role in populating the commonplaces of our lives is difficult to exaggerate. It shapes our sensibilities, our feelings, our knowing, and our affect or lack thereof. Along with these and making use of them are the power of consumerism and the overreach of the nation state. The challenge to the church is one of the faithful formations of the Body of Christ in the face of such pervasive influences and powers as an alternative to them. I believe Hebrew poetry offers the church a model for responding to such challenge in a prophetic way in our time. It involves a commitment of the church to new uses of the electronic commonplaces of our lives in ways that expand the church's sense of God's action in the world and that offer new ways to exercise prophetic witness. We turn here next.

Chapter 10

The Prophetic Use of Figure in Electronic Culture

My interest in Milbank's work relates to the clear implications it has in electronic culture and the emergent multisensory and multimedia rhetoric in our own time. While he discusses the use of figures across history in an oral culture, I work on the place of image, sound, beat, light, move, and dance in an electronic one. How can these possibly be related? I believe they are related in a great many ways. Before we can make these connections we first need a bit of a detour.

Walter Ong argues that *electronic culture is a secondary orality*, meaning that it shares similarities with oral culture. He argues that primary orality and secondary orality are remarkably alike and remarkably unalike. For example, they are alike in their "participatory mystique," their "fostering of a communal sense," their "concentration on the present moment," and their use of "formulas." But they are quite different in that the audiences of electronic culture are much larger, they are more self-consciously and programmatically group-minded. And while primary orality is characterized by people who are "turned outward" (that is, not so oriented to introspection and the focus on subjectivity as we are); secondary orality is characterized by people who turn "outward" because they *"have* turned inward."[1]

Also pertinent in this regard is the work of Scott Lash. He sees the postmodern world as one engaged in a return to image (figure) in contrast to one that is more discursive and based in word. With this comes the devaluation of semantic meaning with the result that the focus is more on the impact of figure than on the dictionary definition or the semantic meaning of words. Hence the young, especially, are far more affected by the experiential than the discursive. They are far more likely to say "That is awesome" than to say "That means a lot." Or, if they use the word *meaning*, it does not suggest semantic elaboration, but that one is touched or moved.[2] Mitchell Stephens describes this situation as "the rise of the image the fall of the word."[3]

I find Lash's work to be unusually helpful. I cannot, of course, do justice to the rich detail of his argument here. Lash is working with Ferdinand de Saussure's analysis of language as signifier (word as sounded, written or printed—*dog*, for example), as signified (the concept—the meaning of a canine or the conceptualization of what a dog is), and referent (an actual object in the world—my dog "Sugar"). His argument is that postmodernity is a de-differentiated "regime of signification." This means that the governing way of using language—signification—is changing. First, the use of language is increasingly figural, not discursive. "To signify via figures rather than words is to signify by the use of icons. Images or other figures which signify iconically do so through their resemblance to the referent" (how much they look like a dog).[4] Second, the division of work in language done by the word and by the concept become less distinguished. They are not differentiated in use; each does not have its own specialized use. Third, this means that words (signifiers) function like things (referents or objects), not like a word in the sense of a semantic concept.

John Milbank and James Bond

I recently experienced this in a quite "figural" way. I am working for the Presbyterian Church, U.S.A. in Louisville. A young man who is the technician for the hotel is helping me connect my computer to the LCD projector and sound system in the ballroom. He asks if I mind if he tightens the connections to my computer with a screwdriver.

"No, I don't mind, but I don't have a screw driver."

"No problem," he says, "I have my James Bond tool with me."

With that he pulls out a highly compact gadget. It has a short ruler, a can opener, a leather gouge, a bottle opener, a long and a short knife blade, a Phillips and a slotted screwdriver, a fingernail file, a fish scaler, and a pair of pliers with wire cutter capacity! Using the slotted screwdriver he tightens the wires to the computer. Meanwhile, I work analytically on what has just transpired. He calls it his "James Bond tool" (a label, but really an image, actually a rather full-blown figure). His label has little to do with conceptualization that would adequately describe the characteristics and functions of this compact piece of hardware. Rather, the figure evokes the films of 007, the spy noted for his high technological capability. The James Bond image suggests the technological resourcefulness of this film hero, although the tool actually is not high tech. But hyperbole is as basic to electronic culture as a way to make things significant as it is to an oral culture to make them memorable.

As he works, I think to myself how I would describe it *conceptually*—and playfully—in terms of my own literate, discursive training. I would call it a light-weight, portable, compact, multi-tool instrument characterized by its versatility in the day-to-day operations of one who has little use for more heavy-duty implement support. It is especially useful for work in audio visual tasks in a hotel that specializes in conferences, seminars, and workshops. Note how conceptual my definition is. Note too that my definition uses highly differentiated language in order to give a more semantic meaning.

See our differences. I call it a highly compact instrument. He calls it a James Bond tool. My label is conceptual, his is figural. My language comes from the differentiated vocabulary of one who has spent a good deal of time with a dictionary; his comes from movies, television, and popular culture. When I try to conceptualize the tool, I resort to complex, conceptual words that attempt to describe its characteristics and functions. He calls attention to a referent by way of a figure. That is, he points to a Hollywood film star and his roles in spy spectacles. My language may be more "accurate," but his is more metaphoric and more interesting. It also has an enormous associational character. (I won't go into those associations here except to say that one must know the grammar—the rules of use—in his language game not to be misled!) His figure can reciprocate and echo through a host of movies and events and more.

As he and I stand there, I cannot help thinking of oral culture and how I would name or characterize his James Bond tool. I decide that in the oral culture I grew up in we would have called it "a damned fancy tool." I can hear someone from that culture characterize it as: "That thing will comb your hair, brush your teeth, and shine your shoes!" Of course, it will not do any of these things literally. Such comments indicate the versatility of the tool. Furthermore, oral cultures do not use words literally about such things, at least not usually; they do them *memorably*, which is different. The hyperbole is meant to be memorable, but it is also meant to convey something of the character of the tool when one does not use language in a literate conceptual way. This usage illustrates something of Milbank's language of ambiguity about things of such concrete makeup, but the ambiguity is relieved by the echoes released by the figure.

So to use the labels—"James Bond tool" and "damned fancy tool"—are remarkably alike but quite different. They are alike because to call that gadget a James Bond tool is also an exercise in hyperbole when thought about in terms of the ultra high tech of 007's instrumentation. Here again the usage is similar but different. The use of "James Bond tool" does not seem so much a usage of hyperbole for the sake of making it *memorable*—we have video to do that—as to make it *significant*, to give it impact. Many electronic products are reproducible and not likely to be lost, at least in the way that an oral performance can be lost if it is not memorable in an oral culture. Rather, the sheer reproducibility and volume of products in an electronic culture make *significance* more of an issue than that of making it remembered.[5]

Finally, Lash argues that in postmodernity the word (signifier) is collapsed into the referent (the thing, an actual object in the "real" world), meaning that the referent functions like a word (like a signifier). That is, James Bond is a figure in one sense—the figure we know through story and spectacle in a film—but he is also a referent, an "actual person" in the movie world. For the young technician James Bond functions as a label (word) but *is* a referent. And in his comment this referent functions like a word.

I think here of the ways that people in motion pictures, TV shows, music videos, and other performers function as signifying referents. For example, the TV show *The Simpsons* provides figures that become referents functioning as signs and not signs representing referents. When a teenager says, "That is so Homer," or, "You are so Bart," meaning that one's actions are so like those of these figures, the teen is using the characters of the show as labels that, indeed, carry content; but it is the use of a referent to carry the "content" of a characteristic rather than words to represent semantically and conceptually that characteristic. In this show comic strip people—truly figures and certainly not even actual people as actors—are referents in terms of their being actual objects as comic strip characters. At the same time they are used in teenage talk as referents.[6]

Figure as Commonplace in Electronic Culture

The point here is that Milbank's discussion of the oral culture of Hebraic poetry has important implications for an electronic culture. To put it far too abstractly, Milbank's discussion of the use of figures across history in Hebraic poetry can be named in the following list.

1. Working with commonplaces;

2. The use of metaphorical figures and images;

3. A rich repetition with variation;

4. The perception of environment and the projection of value;

5. The double play between two poles, neither of which is literal;

6. The location performed in a community with a tradition, with a story; and

7. Copious figures with an abundance of commonplaces.

Along with Milbank the work of Lash needs to be seen in terms of no little "resonance" between his observations on post-modernity and Milbank's on Hebraic poetry. Let me put it in three brief statements:

1. The turn is from the word to the figural, the image;

2. The conceptual is increasingly devalued, and referents gain greater value; and

3. The word increasingly functions as a referent, and the referent functions as a word.

My intention in this section is to take these characteristics from Milbank and Lash and to apply them to electronic culture, especially to multisensory and multimedia rhetoric and to settings of figural ensemble. My purpose is not only as a way to heighten the persuasive powers of contemporary performance, storytelling, and immersion, but also to seek a way to do intrinsically faithful prophetic critique.

First, the character of commonplaces must be reconsidered in an electronic culture. Figures of nature are by no means excluded, but the commonplaces of our culture and our history, especially as those are reconfigured in electronic culture, need also to be considerably expanded. When we realize how central image, sound, beat, light, move, and dance are in our culture, we recognize how commonplace they have become.

To be sure, image, sound, beat, light, move, and dance are not the same as mountain, valley, river, and wilderness in ancient Israel, but they are nevertheless commonplaces. They are also rich in the associations they spring. We do not talk merely about one image, for example, but many. I think of the images of John Kennedy, Jr. I see him as a child in heart-touching salute during the funeral of his famous father. I see him growing up and becoming an extraordinarily handsome young man. Then there are the images of his beginning a magazine and his marriage to be followed by his tragic death. A plethora of moments are caught in photograph and video. His very life seems to begin in tragedy and end there. And yet there is the contradiction of one so seemingly alive and so "having-it-all" but caught between two "bookends" of death.

But young John is not only a "personality," he and others participate in significant events that form the stories of all of our lives. The death of his father, the civil rights movement, King's "I have a dream" speech and his own death, the killing of Bobby, the Vietnam War, the counter culture, the "war" on poverty, the space program, Nixon's recognition of China, his ending of the Vietnam War and his resignation, Gloria Steinem and bell hooks, Jimmy Carter and Ronald Reagan, Jonestown, Nicaragua, AIDS, the destruction of the Berlin Wall, the end of the Soviet Union, the *Challenger* explosion, George Bush and Kuwait, Tiananmen Square, the Clinton years of prosperity and of personal scandal, Columbine and the other school shootings, the election of George W. Bush, watching airplanes fly into the World Trade twin towers, and the wars in Afghanistan and Iraq and their aftermath. These are but a few of the major personalities and events.

Yet, I cannot remember them without "hearing" music I associate with each event. I do not "see" them on TV or in movies only, but hear the music and feel the rhythms that so typically accompany the viewing. Still, the music stands on its own with a rich rhythmic history: Bing Crosby and Frank Sinatra, Judy Garland and Patsy Cline, Elvis Presley and James Brown, Hank Williams and Loretta Lynn, Renata Tebaldi and Leontine Price, Mario Lanza and Luciano Pavarotti, Wilson Pickett and Bruce Springsteen, Dolly Parton and Faith Hill, The Rolling Stones and the Grateful Dead, Jimmy Hendrix and Janis Joplin, Johnny Cash and Garth Brooks, Louis Armstrong and Michael Jackson, Madonna and Jennifer Lopez, Queen Latifah and L.L. Cool J, the Eagles and Eminem, Tina Turner and Beyonce, and the singing of "God Bless America."

I recognize, moreover, thousands of gestures and moves etched in my memory: the nod of John Kennedy's head in a humorous demur, Jackie's grief-stricken poise, the passionate rhythm of King's speeches, the march of astronauts to the rock-et launch, Nixon's arms stretched out beside him with fingers forming a V, Wilma Rudolph's graceful stride, Michael Jackson's moon walk, Jimmy Carter raising his eyebrows, Mickey Hart banging the drums, Michael Jordan dunking a basketball, Bob Hope swinging a golf club on stage, Ronald Reagan's walk, Jerry Rice's choreographic catch of a football, George Bush's "read my lips," fist-pumping Kirk Gibson after a World Series home run, Clinton campaigning, Hillary's pained support of her husband and her celebrative Senate win, Ali's handicapped but poignant gestures in the Olympics, Ricky Martin's Latin moves, the firefighters and the police rushing up the stairs of the World Trade Building to their deaths, the fall of Saddam's statue,

George W. Bush's grin of self-satisfaction, and the frustrated and exasperated signals of U.S. troops in Iraq.

Furthermore, one cannot forget the dances and the dancers: ballet, the jitter bug, the bop, the Hokey Pokey, the striptease, the folkdance, the twist, the line dance, the hustle, the monkey, disco and break dancing, and the tango and the salsa, among many others. And, of course, the dancers: Isadora Duncan and Martha Graham, Shirley Temple and Bo Jangles, Fred Astaire and Gene Kelly, Cyd Charisse and Ginger Rogers, John Travolta and Gregory Hines, Chita Rivera and Gwen Virdon, and Nureyev and Baryshnikov, among many, many others.

These are among the commonplaces of our lives. To be sure we do not share all of them the same way. Many are more generationally specific or more important to different racial and ethnic groups or have more importance because one is male or female. Class is a factor and brings different interpretations to these events. They have different impact because of who one is. Some are only memories learned from movies and TV, but others are among the most telling events of our lives. Some of these are life altering episodes. Others are more amusements or avocational interests, but they are illustrative of the cultural stock, the commonplaces, of our lives.

Frank Rich points out how the 1994 movie *Forrest Gump* effectively captures so much of the experience, the commonplaces, of post–World War II America. The movie is a story of a man with an I.Q. of 75 played by Tom Hanks who winds up "being there" in the significant events of American life from desegregation to Vietnam, from the anti-war movement to the arrest of the Watergate felons, from John Kennedy to John Lennon, and through the times of Kennedy, Johnson, Nixon, Carter, Reagan, Bush, and Clinton. It triggers perceptual memories widely shared by so many in this culture. Further, the young woman Gump loves unrequitedly suffers almost every domestic problem of the times: parental and spouse abuse, alcoholism and addiction to drugs. All of this goes on to the accompaniment of a sound track that includes the "wallpaper of our lives" [my phrase]: "Hound Dog," "Mrs. Robinson," "The Age of Aquarius," "Turn, Turn, Turn," to mention only a few, and features artists such as Tommy James and the Shondells, Aretha, Mama Cass, and the Doors, among others.

Rich maintains the movie is more than a nostalgia trip. Rather, it is the way that audiences identify with Gump. He is a figure "so blank we can project our own dreams onto him." This "turns a clever, manipulative entertainment into something more."[7] Gump lives through the lives of the audience. Rich observes: "His America is shaped by assassins' bullets from Oswald's to Squeaky's to Hinckley's—all of which the movie duly notes—and his personal history reflects the equally violent fallout of his era's proliferating dysfunctional homes."[8] Yet, in the end Gump is not "bitter" or "cynical," but rather is "a healing figure," one ready to leave America's past and his own behind him and "to embrace idealism and hope."[9]

I remember very well not only my own tears, but my surprise that so many were weeping during the film and left the theater wiping their eyes. This is the power of the use of figure, especially across the times of our lives. My interest here is not only my appreciation for the craft and the power of this motion picture, but what we can learn from it about electronic culture and its implications for worship and witness.

I am struck by the way so many events of post–World War II America are placed in the life of Gump, of how they are placed in his story, and how his story becomes our story. This is precisely the kind of rhetoric I have in mind here, only a different story. The issue, as I see it, is to take the events of our lives, to make use of the figures so profoundly related to these events, and then to place them in God's story so that God's story becomes our story. Let me illustrate this two ways.

In Canada they have a holiday much like our Memorial Day here in the states. It is a time to remember those killed in war but also to remember others who have died. In a local church there the membership is made up largely of the G.I. generation (born 1900 to 1924). The pastor decides to remember this generation and its experience. She does a piece in the worship service in which she plays several popular songs from the days of World War II. She says to me: "Tex, I did not glorify war. I simply wanted to bring their memories up in the context of worship so that these could be placed before God." So she plays excerpts from: "White Cliffs of Dover," "Since You Went Away," "I'll Be Seeing You," and "In the Mood," among others.

The pastor is simply blown away by the response. People are weeping quite overtly. The pastor tells me that this is one of the very most significant worship experiences she has ever participated in. At the conclusion of the service one woman in her seventies says to her: "We are taught in church to be concerned about other people and their experience, and we want to do that, but this is the first time I can ever remember that our experience really was lifted up in church." Again, this is done in the context of worship. The experience of a generation is lifted up before God. Such events do not apotheosize a generation. They do not condone the entire lives of a people. They do not turn worship into a sentimental bath of nostalgia. What such events can do is to place lives in God's story. In doing so, there is space for thanksgiving, but also for confession. This becomes a time commonplace figures are placed in liturgy and are both remembered and transformed.

A second illustration comes from Spencer Ebbinga. Spencer has a bachelor's degree in fine arts from the University of Kentucky and works in the Quest Community Church there. A shooting occurs in a local school and he is asked to do a short video for the first Sunday after that tragic event. For this three minute piece Spencer videotapes scenes

151

of students, parents, and friends at the school in deep shock and grief. He also films a local fire capturing something of the burning pain and suffering of the community. One scene is of a young man arrested and handcuffed. Along with these scenes Spencer does video of a sculptor at work with a torch fashioning an art piece in steel. These various scenes are then juxtaposed with guitar and a vocal in the background singing the song "The Hammer Holds" by Bebo Norman. The title of the video is "Starting Over," and suggests that the community can get through these things together.

This artful work faces into the tragedy of the event. It does not dodge the loss or the grief. The video of the building on fire conveys the scalding effect of such senseless death. The poignant moment of a parent being comforted by a friend in a parking lot at the school graphically displays the deep sense of loss by a father and the heart-felt attempts by a friend to say some word or express some form of care to reach out and touch the vast emptiness of a child torn away. At the same time the work of the sculptor conveys the action of God even in tragedies like this one fashioning new ways to be and providing even in this pain the capacity to start over and to go on.

Some may say this is too easy. It depends. If one is formed in the faith, there is no word that can speak to such grief as can the word of God. What is too easy is when the tragedy is not addressed. What is too easy is abstract language that does not face the pain. What is too easy is rosy shibboleths that everything will be OK and that this is God's will. This is what is too easy. But Spencer doesn't do this. I find nothing "easy" in the video. Rather it captures this event in its pain and places it in God's story.[10]

In these two illustrations the events of a congregation's lives are placed in God's story in the context of worship. These events occur in a service where the congregation performs the liturgy and where the commonplaces of members' lives like those of the older people in the church in Canada or events like school shootings in Kentucky are continually raised in relation to God's story. These two kinds of occasions are not brief pieces placed in the midst of a sit-still audience. Rather these are part of a congregation that performs worship in a rich visual context where music and beat and light and move and dance flow with the rhythms of the liturgy and capture the mood and challenge of the events before the congregation's life. These are events within a full blown figural ensemble.

There is no end of the copiousness of occasions like these in our world. Worship that picks up on events like those of the *Challenger* explosion, the collapse of the Berlin Wall, the Oklahoma City bombing, the *Columbia* shuttle disaster, 9/11/01, the Afghanistan and Iraq Wars and a vast range of significant, local happenings and then places them in relation to God's work in the world are exactly the kind of back and forth echoes required if we are to expand and to supplement the practiced understanding of God that enables us to start over and to go on.

In conclusion, in worship and witness we take the figures of our common life, and we place them in the liturgy so that they now echo and reverberate with new import. The world is changed because now a new story encompasses our lives and provides new ways not only to understand but to act in the world. The key questions around the figures of our lives are those of story. Whose story forms and encompasses these figural occasions of our lives? How do we place these in the narrative of faith? Then, further, how do we engage this Story in full figural ensemble? How do image, sound, beat, light, move, and dance serve the Story? And, finally, how do we perform this Story, this figural ensemble in an alternative community of faith? This is the rhetoric I seek here. It is a rhetoric that is intrinsic to the faith and therefore edifying. It is a rhetoric that pitches tent with the culture. This rhetoric can express love both for the culture and its people. It can at the same time be an alternative community that finds itself in opposition to and in heavy critique of that very culture and its people.

To sum up, the work of Milbank demonstrates the use of figure across time in the oral culture of the Hebrew prophets. The use of natural commonplaces like mountains, valleys, rivers, and wilderness take on a figural character and are used metaphorically to suggest the relationship of God to history and to the world. Further, these commonplaces, repetitiously used but with changing variety to fit new occasions, echo back and forth together building a cumulative prophetic effect. In doing so they clarify and amplify the understanding of God's action in the life of Israel. Copious as they are, they are a rich resource for a community of faith in its self-understanding and in the development of its tradition, especially as they are performed in and by a community. These figures then become in human terms an inexhaustible reservoir of practiced meaning.

Next, I suggest that electronic culture shares some similarity with oral culture, especially in the use of referents and figures to communicate in nonliteral ways. Figure as referent takes hold of many of the signifying functions of words. I then draw attention to the myriads of images, music, beat, light, move, and dance in our lives and the ways these are commonplaces for our self-understanding and for locating our place in the world. These, however, are set in competing stories. I argue for worship where God's story is performed in immersive practices as an alternative to the culture and where direct opposition to the culture is assumed.

The task now is to examine ways that critique can be done in these immersive events. They are not settings given to the critical distance of the print world. How, then, does criticism take place in figural ensemble. In the next chapter I contend that the challenge is to learn the practices of critical immersion.

154

Chapter 11

Critical Immersion

I do about fifty events a year as a lecturer, preacher, and work-shop leader around the United States, Canada, and overseas. I have done these kinds of speaking and seminar engage-ments now for thirty-five years. Over the past fifteen years or so I have noticed a change in the groups I work with, and I see this change happening to other speakers with whom I share programs in these events. When a speaker enters into a critical stance on a social issue, a kind of "flattening" or "deadening" of the audience occurs. To change the metaphor, you can see "the shades being drawn down behind the eyeballs" of those gathered.

I think of one exception to this. When a speaker is "cheer-leading" a group with more intellectual interests, this is not typically the case. By "cheerleading" I mean addressing an audience of people of a common mind who agree with the speaker. When the audience, however, is more diverse and more reflective of the population in general and of a less intel-lectual bent, the deadening or the disengagement occurs.

I am convinced that this happens for at least two reasons. The first reason is that we have overdone the "hermeneutics of sus-picion." People grow tired of the constant nay-saying that goes on. They are sick of the constant "negativism," as they often say. I do not know for sure where all the roots of this lie. Some of it is doubtless tied to the excessive criticism that occurs.

It is also tied to the kind of fragmentation in the culture where so much of everyday life does not come together. Just one example, if the parents both work outside the home—even more so if it is a single parent—and the kids are in school, the daily grind of putting all that together is exhausting. This is especially so when one of the kids is sick or angular discord between the school and the family or problems at work are not being resolved or other issues intervene. Who wants to go to a workshop and hear criticism of a host of other issues while struggling just to put everyday life together?

Somewhere in all of this people look for a "hermeneutics of affirmation." They look for good news. They hardly need to be told that things are bad. They want something that is uplifting. This is not escapism. It is cultural weariness. To ignore it is rhetorical suicide. But it is worse than not being "heard"; it is cruelty. There is real trouble out there, and major discontent. To have nothing more than "critique" to offer is like throwing acid on a sunburn. Critical cheerleading at the pep rallies of intellectuals—right, middle, and left—does not address the vast majority of the American people. The critique that can raise the important questions must occur in the context of affirmation. It is not just sound rhetoric; it is rightly "speaking" good news.

The second reason is what Lawrence Grossberg sees as a disconnect between the worldviews of people and their energy. We hold "positions" on issues, but we are not motivated by them. Grossberg describes this as a "disarticulation, at specific sites, of the relationship between ideology and affect, of investment and meaning, as two intertwined constitutive dimensions of human exchange."[1] This disconnect is not merely a psychological phenomenon, but a cultural one.

Another way to say this is that what is important is not significant and what is significant is not important. That is, what is important, what really matters does not have the feeling, the affect behind it to do something with it or about it. Meanwhile the significant—what touches us, what has impact on us, what moves us to action—does indeed draw our energy, but is not important.

I remember some years back watching—and I do mean watching—a stadium of some fifty thousand people standing, singing, dancing, in a multisensory and multimedia event led by a nationally popular artist. Percussive and moving lights bathe them in rapid beat and sweeping illumination. They are surrounded by the sound and beat of an overwhelming P.A. system. Huge screens display moving images of the artist, the band, and the crowd. They are all performers fully engaged in this environment, this ecology of celebration. They are captivated.

And they are singing "Achy Breaky Heart."

I have no wish to be a moralizing bluenose who can see no value in a playful event, but I do believe we have something to learn about critique in both the event and the contradiction Grossberg names. I find Grossberg's insight most helpful when examined as the difference between the practices of importance and the practices of significance.

By practices of importance I mean those practices that are intrinsically valuable. In terms of the church these practices are worship, Eucharist, prayer, evangelism, justice, and peace, to provide a short list. These are the practices that count in the church's life before God. Practices intrinsic to God's story, that are instances of it, and through which the church loves God and the world, are of the utmost importance in the church's life.

By practices of significance I mean those practices in a given historical period that have impact, that touch and move people. These are the practices that persuade, that take on a certain aesthetic appeal, that call forth desire and express energy and passion in powerful ways. More than mere preferences of people, these practices reflect the way people are "wired," the ways they are culturally constructed.

The practices of significance change over time. One important way that they change is when the basic communication patterns of a society change. For example, in an oral culture, which existed throughout much of the church's history, the practices of significance are decidedly oral in form. The capacity to make a word or an event memorable is central, so hyperbole or overstatement is crucial in an oral culture. Hence Jesus can say, "If you say to this mountain, 'Be taken up and thrown into the sea.'" With the coming of print, however, these practices change. The point is that in other times the church has found ways to integrate the practices of importance with the practices of significance.

In our time these practices have already changed, at least among younger generations. In the emergent culture the practices of significance are very different from those of print. Furthermore, as Grossberg reports, because of these changes a breakdown has occurred between the practices of importance and those of significance.[2]

These things, then, the weariness with the hermeneutics of suspicion and the hunger for a hermeneutics of affirmation, on the one hand, and the disconnect between what is important and what is significant, on the other, represent major barriers to prophetic critique.

But prophetic criticism is too crucial to let go because the times are resistant to it. What is required is critique that occurs in a context of affirmation and that reconnects the practices of importance with those of significance. We need to move beyond the practices of critique as formed in print culture to an emergent form of critique in an electronic world.

From Critical Distance to Critical Immersion

Let's look first at critique in terms of the form it takes in literate practices, especially in the modern period. Critique is understood as critical *distance*. In reading one stands back from the text. That is, one backs off from the page to see what the author writes on page 18 and then on page 151 to see if these agree, or how she got from the point on page 18 to the point on page 151. The critical reader "looks on" and asks throughout a reading "can it be otherwise than the point the author makes?"

Frederic Jameson argues, however, that "distance in general (including 'critical distance' in particular) has very precisely been abolished" in the emergent society he calls postmodern. He states flatly, "We are submerged in its henceforth filled and suffused volumes" to the point that we cannot get "the big picture" [my term]. This submersion has taken hold even of our understanding of nature and has penetrated and colonized our desire.[3] Cultural submersion engulfs critical distance.

As a result, Jameson is concerned about the "spatial disorientation" of people in contemporary postmodern society. We are not able "to get the big picture" of what is going on and to understand the cultural captivity, the economic exploitation and the political oppression of late capitalism. We are not able to locate ourselves, to position ourselves, to see ourselves within the "new decentered communication networks of capitalism." This absence of a big picture hinders the capacity of people to organize, to resist, and to take action against the powerful forces at work.

I find Jameson's analysis to this point quite compelling. His sense of the ways we are submerged in networks of the electronic culture of the new capitalism may be overstated but not for that reason unreal. He sees us too much trapped in a culture of images and simulacra that envelops us in a vast hyper-reality that is "realer than real" in Baudrillard's terms. Yet, if he overstates the case, there is much in his claims that rings true and troubling.

One important response to the submersion Jameson addresses is to turn to critical immersion. Such a turn does not mean there is no place for critical distance, but it does mean to learn a new set of practices. The way to challenge the submersion of today's consumer capitalism is to counter with a different and oppositional alternative. The submersion in which we are caught requires immersion in a different story, engaged in practices intrinsic to this story and one embodied in the performance of a different community. This challenge will take place most persuasively through multisensory and multimedia figural ensemble.

Critical immersion is a different set of practices than that of critical distance, though there are certainly parallels between them. The rest of this chapter attempts to lay out basic practices in critical immersion and their role in the life of the community of faith. I focus here primarily on worship, though these practices are not limited only to worship.

Basic Practices in Critical Immersion

Placement in Story and the Hermeneutics of Affirmation

The first step in critical immersion is the use of figural ensemble to embody God's story. That is, image, sound, beat, light, move, and dance serve to instantiate the narrative of faith. By this I do not mean to place God's story in figural ensemble, but to place figural ensemble in God's story. Multisensory and multimedia rhetoric serve the story and not the other way around.

What this does is to reconnect the practices of importance with those of significance. The church is blessed and missioned with the practices of importance: worship, baptism, Eucharist, evangelism, justice, peace, and more. Furthermore, the import of all of these practices of faithfulness is basically one of good news. The central message and final word of faith is *Yes!* Figural ensemble thus addresses the practices of significance and the hermeneutics of affirmation. So what is proposed is the performative enactment of God's good news by means of figural ensemble.

But in the church today such practices are largely absent. Rather worshipers are often overwhelmed by long renditions of "talking heads," by music with beat and style out of previous centuries, by passive audiences not active congregations, by literate practices of reading the liturgy rather than a more fully embodied performance of it, and all of this too often in visually, aurally, and illuminatively impoverished settings. And, should the people physically move, the dead would rise!

Let me be clear. I am not suggesting that the church do what I call "Boomer worship." That is, sing six praise songs none of which is connected to the other, that are interspersed with comments by some fifty-something, "spiritual guru" who thinks he (usually) is an undiscovered rock star. These songs are then followed by two Bible verses and a didactic sermon. This trivial violation of Christian liturgy and tradition engages neither the practices of significance nor those of importance. I hasten to say that most Boomers have no use for it either. Put services of this ilk together over several years and hell becomes a washboard road of backbeat bump, bump, bump.

Worship in the setting I envision here is quite traditional, not in the sense of being staid and deadly, but in the sense that the worship will be formed by the Christian year, by Scripture, by classic structures of worship, and by the centrality of the Eucharist, but all of these using figural ensemble. In terms of the Christian year we need as the church to breathe the time of God's story. In America we breathe too much the time of the nation state; and the Christian year often gets inserted as an afterthought, when it is not actively overtaken by the consumerization of Christmas and Easter. On one thing I am clear. When I die, the American eagle will not swoop down, grab me by the backside, and take me to eternal life. Most people in the church understand this. We need to play out the implications of this understanding in terms of relativizing the nation state in its time and by the constructive formation of the community of faith in God's time. This means breathing Christian time.

Further, worship in these settings will use either the lectionary or some other suitable substitute that gets the Scripture before the congregation over the course of three years or so. I do not mean readings only by talking heads. My friend Eric Elnes presents Scripture by means of images, visual display, music and beat, video, artistic expression such as painting and sculpture, and dance and other forms for the performance of the text.[4] This does not, of course, exclude reading, but it places it in a synthesis of figural display and action.

Furthermore, I see such liturgy composed of the classic structures of worship such as that of gathering, proclamation and response, Eucharist, and sending forth. I mention above how the children can provide images for the time of gathering. In terms of proclamation and response I envision liturgical acts such as confessions, affirmations of faith, biblical "readings," offerings, and sermons as far more multisensory and multimedia in form. These can be sung, placed in drama, or danced while engaged in visually rich encounter.

The Eucharist is central to such worship. Along with baptism it is the most multisensory of the practices of worship. Saint Gregory of Nyssa Episcopal Church in San Francisco enacts the Eucharist in reading and dance, in song and drummed rhythm. While not using screens and images, at least in my experience with them, the service is nonetheless quite rich visually in costume and color, in icons of saints on the wall, and in wonderfully textured hangings and other works of art.

Figural ensemble in worship changes the sermon, but certainly does not eliminate it. It is now an event in a more multisensory, multimedia environment. It will draw from the resources of image, sound, beat, light, move, and dance. The Word is not only spoken but performed. It is not only preached but enacted. I do not mean merely putting the outline of the sermon on a screen, but embedding the word in multisensory and multimedia event. It is more interactive. It is more narrative. It is less an intellectual argument of discursive elaboration but rather, as Leonard Sweet says, the construction of an experience.[5] The key throughout worship is to place the premium on performance of the liturgy by the congregation, and that in figural ensemble.

Such liturgy does not exclude silence. There is nothing more multisensory than the absence of sound. To place silence rightly in the liturgy is intrinsic to our being before God and fits the worship, praise, and celebration of God's story. Worship, moreover cannot be reduced to a multimedia sprint filled with nothing but hard, fast, backbeat music with percussive light and active movement and dance. Classic liturgies have their own flows. They can, indeed, pulse with the full throat, the embodied dance, and celebratory praise of gratitude for all that God has done and does. They can exult in the ecstasy of God's presence. Yet, classic liturgies also move into pensive moments of confession and prayer. To be still and know that God is God is a multisensory act and can be served by multimedia. My point here is to lift up the importance of silence and to be clear that liturgy itself has a rhythm and flow. Figural ensemble can serve that flow.

To do what I envision requires a motivated practice of production. The congregation itself will be deeply involved in the planning, the preparation, and construction of the service. This is important for many reasons. Let me name just a few. It prevents the figural ensemble from being the work of an elite. It reduces the likelihood of manipulation. It involves rich education in the faith when people struggle, for example, to turn a biblical text into a multimedia presentation. Production in these ways is an exercise in formation. We are edified in these actions. In other words, we are built up; we are formed as the people of God by the practices of liturgical production.

Further, it brings into play a large number of people whose gifts and graces, even at an amateur level, are not often used in the preparation and performance of worship. I still remember with pain the woman who told me, "I am a professional dancer, and I have never been invited by my congregation to share my gift in worship or to teach others to do so." More positively, I think of the excitement of children doing art work each week in Sunday school in which they express in their wonderful, primal ways the church year. Then they gain a sense of their own work in the liturgy when they see their images used in worship as praise of God. For example, I can imagine the use of forty to fifty images done by the children that present the theme of Advent during the gathering time of worship.

This production will require teams of people, not just a few individuals. A congregation needs a dance team, a drama team, a band, a light team, a team devoted to finding or making images, a team that scours popular culture and other venues for material to be used in The Story. Such teams are porous, meaning that their boundaries are permeable and that individuals can move in and out of them freely so that "new life" can bring fresh thought and skill and so that the few are not "burned out" into passivity.

The worship team provides the planning and coordination of these groups and puts the final service together. While some people despair of finding this kind of motivation, I discover, however, that when these teams are made up of people for whom such work centers in their gifts and graces as an expression of their vocation, great energy comes forth. To be sure, there will be false starts. Life circumstances change, and people move in and out of the teams. Some fail and disappoint, and others find they do not have the desire; but these are characteristic of life itself. They are not specific only to the worship here envisioned. These problems can be addressed.

This is only a taste of what it means to place figural ensemble in God's story and to work fundamentally from a hermeneutic of affirmation. Also, affirmation is fundamental to critique. For the church this yes is God's story. Any critique by the church begins in this good news, indeed, takes its grounding from this affirmation of life before God.

With this understood, we can move more directly to specific forms of critical immersion. The first of these is the critical form of taking one story and putting it in another.

Putting the World's Story in God's Story

Closely related to the construction of a hermeneutics of affirmation is the notion of putting the world's story in God's story. This critical tactic is akin to what Miss Harriet Annette Buehl does to Mr. Archon as reported in the first chapter. She is able to place the racist story in God's story and undo it. The focus here is to do this kind of narrative turn in the context of the figural ensemble of a worship service.

As we see in the previous chapter, figural ensembles generate ecological, environmental settings in which people are immersed. Worship, then, is the performative enactment of God's story. In such settings a basic form of prophetic critique is the introduction of positions, issues, acts, and other events that so clearly violate the "world" of God's story. To place these violative, oppressive, exploitative, and destructive events and commitments in God's story is to place them under serious critique.

These critical forms do not have to be heavy-handed or lacking in humor. My best recent experience with placing one story critically in another is the annual assembly of the Valley

Interfaith Project (VIP) here in Phoenix. The VIP is a metro-politanwide, really statewide, community organizing effort. The attendance at this meeting is fifteen hundred people. It is a festive event in a crowded convention center. A mariachi band gives musical atmosphere. Some of the people dress in traditional Mexican costumes. Churches are there with signs and banners; placards appear throughout the room, and friends and acquaintances greet each other. It is a happy and celebrative time. While there are no screens, which would add greatly to the event, nevertheless it is a highly visual experi-ence. While Mexican music and beat vitalize the ethos, there is no dancing, but active clapping and movement embody the rhythm of the action.

More than a dozen politicians sit on the platform having been invited to respond to a number of quite pointed ques-tions regarding their support of the VIP agenda. These ques-tions are to be asked in front of the crowd by VIP leadership as the climax of the meeting.

The most effective moment of the event is the drama per-formed by two fourteen-foot-high puppets on stilts who play the role of corrupt Arizona politicians. With big false-face heads of a caricatured sort, they walk out before the crowd to the accompaniment of a great parody of fanfare. Miked, they then sing to the tune of a popular song lyrics about the ways that the electorate can be hustled and used, and about how they can serve powerful interests without their constituents knowing it, especially the housing development powers that be. It is done humorously so that it contributes to the festivity of the occasion; but the puppets are dealing with serious issues, and everyone knows it. Though the song by these "politicians" is an overstated dramatization, it nevertheless reflects very real attitudes and the special interest character of much legislative action in Arizona. The crowd responds uproariously, laughing in all the right places, applauding and shouting, but keenly aware of the gravity of the situation humorously explored.

To place this drama in the context of a broad cross-section of grassroots people whose very organization is based on democratic principle and process is to place the story of a politics of greed in the story of a politics of the people. Hardly anything can be more effectively heard. To put it in a multisensory and multimedia setting of this kind is to engage in graphic, performative, enacted critique. By the time the politicians are brought to the lectern to respond to the agenda of VIP, the crowd is ready, and the politicians are "informed."

Worship in the church will not usually take this shape. That is, I do not see a dozen politicians sitting behind the pulpit waiting for a time to be questioned by the pastor after a compelling parody of legislators bought off by powerful special interests. Other ways of using this form of critique are appropriately available. For example, a worship service done in figural ensemble can form its work around the Magnificat of Mary in Luke, passages from the prophets, and from James 2:1-14. It can address the impact of so-called "welfare reform" that pushes single mothers out of the home to do minimum wage jobs while their preadolescent children fend for themselves. It can highlight the thousands of mentally ill people put on the streets because of lack of funding. These issues can appropriately occur in a service devoted centrally to an affirmation of the reign of God. It can, indeed, be a service that envisions the full completion of nature and history. At the same time in song, drama, video, and in dance the concrete lived stories of real people can be placed in God's story and our hope for God's reign.

Ecology and Fit

For ten years my friend Monica Eppinger has been an employee of the State Department. She tells about an event in the basement of a department store in the old Soviet Union before its breakup. The city is Leningrad. At this store when business hours ended, certain salesclerks agreed to lock up. Just before closing time young adults came into the store in twos and threes and hid behind clothes racks. Others were let in after hours by the employees who stayed late.

They then gather in the basement, and it becomes a space where young adults celebrate and dance. The band is a group of classically trained musicians who form a rock band but mainly play jazz in these settings. The lead singer—really the lead shouter—reads loudly from the writings of Marx and Lenin to jazz accompaniment. It is a sharply critical and subversive act because these readings stand in such sharp contrast to what the Soviet government actually does. By reading from Marx and Lenin, however, the shouter is able to avoid imprisonment. Even so, Monica reports that there really is no public place to do such things. The state parks are under too much surveillance, and other venues are too risky. So they find a space in the basement of this store.

What is interesting here is that the Soviet government is never mentioned. It is the "elephant in the room" that everyone knows is there but is never overtly named. Yet the message is clear, but it is more than a message. It is the performance of an alternative "reality," it is living in a different order, in a different "world." It is, moreover, clear that this enacted world is in sharp opposition to that of the Soviet government.

This is never a concert-hall crowd, never a big gathering because there is not enough space in the basement; but it is crowded. The music is a kind of free jazz and therefore unpredictable. The crowd's response to the singer/shouter is not that of call and response as in the Black church. It is more of an improvisational, unpatterned engagement. It resembles more the spontaneity of a Pentecostal church, Monica says.

Yet, it is very effective. "If you can imagine Bob Dylan shouting the Pledge of Allegiance in opposition to war, you get some idea of the character and mood of the event," says Monica. It also has a kind of punk element, she says. It is quite "provocative and subversive," and "it really resonated with the people."

Events like this one illustrate an immersive event of an environmental kind. The basement of a store becomes another reality. Michel de Certeau speaks of how the powerful build *places* to display their control and authority. Meanwhile, the powerless set up *spaces* in the midst of the places to resist this captivity.[6] What a fitting space to do so in the basement of a store. Note too how this event and the readings from Marx and Lenin fly in the face of the realities outside that setting. The actions of the Soviet government are alien to the ecology of that basement oppositional and alternative "world." They fit neither the reality enacted and performed in the basement nor the visions articulated by Marx and Lenin.

It is no great leap to learn from this practice the ways that God's story in worship is an instantiation of a multisensory, multimedia world, one where alien stories are set in sharp discontinuity with the faith. The point is that immersive events create an ecology, an environment. One of the most sharply critical practices in such settings is to introduce—even implicitly as is the case here—things that do not fit, that are alien to or violate that ecology.

The Scottsdale Congregational United Church of Christ has a worship service it calls The Studio. It is a multisensory, multimedia, experientially oriented service that generates the kind of environmental setting envisioned here. Radonna Bull does multimedia presentations for The Studio. In a worship service before the war with Iraq in 2003 Radonna developed a video built around images from a demonstration in Phoenix against the war. These images were embedded with phrases from

Luke 6 such as "Love your enemies," "To him who strikes you on the cheek, offer the other also."

The biblical text is placed in a moving montage of animations, photographs of the demonstration, and pictures from the news. Placards and Scripture appear side by side. The signs vary greatly in their messages: "Pray for peace," "Peace is not made by killing other people's children," "Peace is patriotic," "Blessed are the peacemakers," "Who would Jesus bomb?" "How did *our* oil get under *their* sand?" "Osama wants war too," and "Duct tape your ass goodbye." The music is the Rolling Stones' "Street Fightin' Man" with a heavy rock beat, and the images are timed to occur and change with the rhythm.[7] It is a percussive, visual, rhythmic experience that engages the clapping and movement of the congregation.

The scriptural passages in the video are the biblical "readings" for that Sunday. It occurs in a worship service that is multisensory and multimedia throughout. It is a service where classical structures of worship shape the liturgy and where the Eucharist is celebrated every week.

I do understand that it is difficult for most church leadership to do a piece this prophetic in many churches. It is testimony to the ongoing ministry of the pastor and key lay leadership that the Scottsdale Church is able to be this forthright. It is also testimony to the kind of multisensory rhetoric that operates in the church Sunday after Sunday. It has done so now for more than four years. The congregation comes expecting this kind of worship and with some frequency this kind of prophetic critique. One basic form of this critique is the introduction into the "ecology" of The Studio presentations that do not fit the reality of the gospel.

Juxtaposition

A fourth form of critique is the use of juxtaposition. Here I have in mind the placing of two items side by side as a form of critique as in Wittgenstein's approach to philosophy. His approach does not develop a position, but rather attempts to be therapeutic, that is, to change the way we look at or engage things. Really, it seeks to change our sensibilities. In his descriptions of the ways to do this, Wittgenstein makes use of "objects of comparison," or juxtaposition. Placing things side by side can change the way we look at things. Wittgenstein sees us engaging the world through basic images, really the paradigmatic images through which we view the world. Or, in a more kinesthetic metaphor, not visual, he speaks of something like a "trusting grasp."[8] In other words, it is not merely the objects we see but the lenses through which we see the world. Or to change the visual metaphor, it is the trusted ways in which we grasp or engage the world. These can be changed through objects of comparison. That is, to juxtapose things is to get a new perspective. It breaks the authority of certain images and figures over our lives. We are released from the captivity of these images and figures.[9]

As we find throughout this book, we have not only paradigmatic images, but paradigmatic music, sonic beat, lighting practices, and bodies formed by patterns of movement and dance. We also are captured in stories that shape the way we understand and live in the world. Prophetic critique challenges these captivities. So my concern is to work with figural juxtaposition as a basic tactic for reconstructing our sensibilities.

The movie *Bowling for Columbine* is a case study in this form of critique. Almost every part of the movie is a juxtaposition of one event or scene with another. One part is entitled "Wonderful World." This section opens with an interview with a public relations official of Lockheed Martin, the world's largest weapons maker and the largest employer in Littleton, Colorado, the city where Columbine School is located and where the shootings occured in 2001. The PR official is standing in front of large missiles under construction in the factory.

Michael Moore, the filmmaker, asks the PR official why school shootings happen. He answers that he doesn't know, but suggests it is related to a range of issues teens experience around anger. He reports that Lockheed Martin gave $100,000 to anger management training for the school students. Moore states that perhaps the students do not see much difference in their dads going off to make weapons of mass destruction and shooting kids at school. The PR executive states that he does not see that connection. He sees Lockheed Martin building weapons to protect the United States from aggressive nations that attempt to do harm to us. He maintains that we don't do that, act aggressively toward other nations.

With this comment the movie turns to a series of scenes of the sordid history of the United States in its aggressive actions against certain nations. The background music is Louis Armstrong singing "It's a Wonderful World," but on the screen are a series of pictures—some quite gruesome—displaying events in which the United States has been deeply involved. Among these are the assassination of Prime Minister Mossadeq of Iran in 1953 and the installation of the Shah. It moves through our assisting in the assassination of Allende and the bringing to power of Pinochet. It depicts briefly our actions in El Salvador, Iran, Nicaragua, Panama, and others. It especially reports our giving three billion dollars to train and arm Osama bin Laden in the 1980s. It calls attention to our support of the Taliban in Afghanistan and our funding and support of Saddam Hussein in Iraq. The film ends with the attack on the World Trade Towers in New York on 9/11/01. As each of the pictures is displayed, the screen lists how many civilians were killed in these episodes. The juxtaposition of "It's a Wonderful World" is a graphic testimonial contrast to specific instances of national shame over the past fifty years.

This excerpt from the movie can be used directly in a worship service devoted to the Christian commitment to peace.

Its incorporation into a figural ensemble of songs, biblical presentations, prayers of confession and recommitment, sermonic interpretation, and as fundamentally alien to the Eucharist offer a different construction of the "world" to counter, to actively oppose these policies and actions of the United States, and to offer alternative ways to be God's people.

Other Strategies

These four practices strike me as especially important in the use of critical immersion by the church in ways intrinsic to God's story. Yet, these are certainly not exhaustive. Let me mention briefly a few forms of critique I learned from Michel Foucault.[10] First is the tactic of making the familiar unfamiliar. As a college sophomore I first learned that the Bible is culturally conditioned. It changed my entire orientation to the biblical text. At that time I was unfamiliar with Calvin's notion of God speaking "baby talk" with us. Rather, I became a child of the Enlightenment in which I saw myself as some free individual able to assess "objectively" the "primitive notions" and "myths" of scripture in the light of a "capacious reason." In these years I did not see myself merely standing on some Archimedean point—a neutral and objective perspective—indeed, I was "strolling on an Archimedean veranda."

Later I learned that I too am culturally conditioned (!) and that reason is tradition dependent. This completely defamiliarized my sophomoric "position" and crumbled my Archimedean "foundation." I was forced to reexamine my orientation to the Scripture and to raise sharp questions about which story operates through me. I did not thereby become a fundamentalist, but I found myself taking the Scripture far more seriously and attempting to read it faithfully as a member of the Body of Christ and not as some fictional free individual who stands above history by the power of some unconditioned "reason."

The point is that such defamiliarization forms of critique are profound in their impact. They can be placed significantly in immersive events of figural ensemble.

A second form of critique is to "problematize" the status quo as an eternal and self-evident order. Foucault does this by demonstrating how a given situation emerges historically. That is, a given state of affairs is not the way things have always been, but rather comes to be at a certain time under certain conditions and is not the way things must be. This kind of critique is especially open to figural ensemble because of the many ways that images and video can be used to make the case, especially when backed with music, sonic logic, lighting, movement and dance.

Closely related to this is a third tactic, that of demonstrating the way "nature of" arguments function. That is, when someone says that you can't do anything about a certain problem because it is just the nature of things; this is just the way things are. This is a "nature of" argument. It invests a status quo with "reality" so that the status quo is preserved. But this is exactly the point: "nature of" arguments serve privilege and protect the way things are. They typically serve established power. Figural ensemble with its capacity to place such arguments in other stories, to place them in the acids of a more faithful ecology, and to juxtapose them with different "realities" demonstrates that they are not "natural" or necessary.

There are a good many other tactics that can be faithfully used by figural ensemble: the display of dominating forces acting behind supposedly "neutral" and beneficent facades, and the exposure of the political violence of institutions that defend their policies as "responsible" or even supportive of the common good. Figural ensemble, moreover, can be an effective way to listen to subjugated voices and to hear into speech those stymied and gagged by the principalities and powers.

In sum and conclusion, critical immersion is the emergent form of critique in an electronic culture. This does not spell the end of critical distance. For one thing it is helpful in thinking through and learning the practices of critical immersion. I do believe, though, that critical immersion is far more effective than critical distance with the great sweep of the people of the United States and other countries increasingly characterized by electronic culture. It is central to a new rhetoric. Furthermore, the church is especially positioned to make use of this form of critique because of its base in the good news of God's story. It can place the necessary hermeneutic of suspicion in a compelling and more encompassing hermeneutic of affirmation. In this way the church can reunite the practices of significance with those of importance. This new form of critique in the church, however, requires learning a new range of critical practices in immersive settings and building the capacity to address the stories and claims of the world in figural ensembles intrinsic to faithful witness and worship.

It is time now to pull this effort together and draw this work to a close, first with a summary of this effort and then with description of what I envision in a worship service.

Epilogue

We live today in a massive turning of culture. In history we see cultures change from those of oral communication to those of print. In our own time the shift is from a typographical world to an electronic and digital one. This certainly does not mean the end of print. It does mean that print now occurs in a new context and that a new culture is not only in the making but is already here in its early formative period.

In changes of this magnitude the shift is not merely one of a change of communicative patterns. These kinds of transformations reconstruct and reconfigure the ways we know, the structure of our feeling, and the forms of our bonding and commitment. With such pervasive shifts come complex new practices. These practices are not mere activities in which we engage, but rather are formative of our very lives. They change who we are.

In times like these new stories emerge that form and ground life. Meanwhile old stories change or die. This is especially true of stories that cannot adequately encompass the new forms of life and/or cannot take on practices of significance that touch and impact the lives of people. In the United States especially, but increasingly in the larger world, the stories of the nation state and of consumer capitalism become pervasive, life-orienting stories. The capacities of the one to claim idolatrous devotion and of the other to commodify life—with its own idolatrous forms—are major threats in our common lives.

To challenge these stories is basic to the witness of the church; but the church too must face into the history-altering events of our time, especially the transformation of communications, the emergence of recent forms of multisensory and multimedia persuasion, and the rise of new practices of significance. Furthermore, since worship is the central act of congregations and the principal means by which unchurched people make their early contacts with the communities of faith, the capacity of the church to "pitch tent" with these practices is basic to its negotiating a relationship to the emergent culture.

Yet, the church can lose its soul in attempting to translate the gospel into the language and practices of a culture. I propose as the alternative to this that the church get its own story right and that it serve God's story. Basic to this is engaging in practices that are intrinsic to that story. Still, the church must "pitch tent" with the wider culture. Here my contention is that the practices of the culture be used to serve God's story and not the other way around.

The focus here is principally on multisensory and multimedia rhetoric in venues where "audiences" perform with artists in highly immersive events that take on an environmental character. These are the most powerful forms of rhetoric at work in the culture today. These events not only communicate and persuade, they form our bodies, our minds, and our commitments. They shape the cognitive, cathectic, evaluative, and bonding makeup of people's lives. For the church, then, the question becomes one of how these new indigenous practices of rhetoric can be placed in God's story so that they serve that story rather than become the occasion for the church to sell out and conform to the principalities and powers.

The use of multisensory and multimedia rhetoric requires a craft knowing of the uses of image, sound, beat, light, move, and dance in the emergent culture and how they serve in the representation and presentation of God's story. These figural ensembles involve a capacity to synthesize and integrate sensory experience in an atmospheric and ecological practice. This is the future of worship in the church and is a basic form of its witness in the days to come.

Practices of this kind do not abandon the tradition of the church. The emergent practices are to serve the tradition, not excise it. So worship is constituted by "breathing" the Christian year, by classic structures of the liturgy, by biblical "readings," by the Word "preached," and by the centrality of the Eucharist. This is no sit-still audience merely looking and listening, but the Body of Christ celebrating, confessing, praying, singing, dancing, and enacting the worship of God. The congregation performs this rich traditional liturgy.

Liturgy of this kind takes into worship life the commonplaces and events of our time. It recognizes that the prophetic work of clarification and supplementation of God's story requires an ongoing echo between what happens in the world and what God is doing there. The prophetic work of the church must also take on the responsibility of critique, but now it is a critical immersion taking place in an atmospheric environment of God's story. It is critical immersion in an immersive affirmation.

This is the vision of worship and witness I articulate in these pages. It represents a major change for the great majority of churches in the United States, including those that are already engaged in "contemporary worship." What we need is faithful experimentation not only to learn the craft of this kind of liturgy and witness but to discover the range of ways this can be done. This experimentation has begun in some churches. In my experience, however, it has not been done in very many places on the scale envisioned here. This work needs to begin.

To close, then, let me share my dream for my own congregation. Peggy and I are active in the Asbury United Methodist Church in Phoenix, Arizona. It is a central city multiracial, multiclass congregation with a membership that is about half gay and lesbian with a good many people who are in recovery through Twelve Step programs. The church, a dying congregation when Pastor Jeff Procter-Murphy arrived on the scene ten years ago, began to build and grow again because of its active welcoming efforts. The church's statement of purpose says it well: "A place for all people to make disciples of Jesus Christ." We are not a large congregation, with a membership of about 180 and an average attendance of a total of 150 at two services.

The congregation uses media well. We work with projector and screen, and Bob McBane oversees the tech booth and trains others to work with him. Our pastor is not only an excellent preacher but is technologically competent and distinguishes carefully between good contemporary music and the fluff. The liturgy is classically informed and makes generous use of images, video, and music with beat. It has been the best worship experience of my life on an ongoing week by week basis. Furthermore, we celebrate the Eucharist at both services on Sunday morning. To see this wide cross section of people receiving bread and wine is a foretaste of the Reign of God. The worship, the sermon, indeed, the service is prophetic in the way issues and commonplaces of the day are raised week by week. We are, moreover, prophetic, in another sense, by the very fact of who we are.

Presently we work with a small screen (about 6 by 8 feet) placed at the back of the chancel. With a screen this small the engagement with it is more of an absorptive practice than an immersive one. The seating arrangement is one where the congregation partly faces each other but not completely. It is interactive but can be much more so.

So here is my dream. I envision a rearrangement of the seating so that the rows of moveable chairs face the communion table in the center of the room. The sanctuary is a good-sized rectangular space with good width that will support an arrangement of seating of four long elliptical rows of chairs on each side of the room creating worship in the round. This will make the congregation quite interactive with people directly facing each other.

Epilogue

I envision two screens just above the congregation's heads on both sides of the room. These need to be about 8 by 10 feet so that we do not see them "down there" as in the chancel, but rather we are immersed in them and with the people of God. The line of sight shifts very slightly in moving back and forth from congregation to screen. I see praise team and piano, bass, and drums at one end of the seating arrangement with the pastor leading and preaching from the other end.[1]

As I say, we already make good use of images and video, but this new arrangement will make them far more immersive. The contemporary music is quite good, carefully selected with sound lyrics and diverse rhythm. Barbara Catlin is our able pianist. We need more musicians on a regular basis, a financial issue; but improved stewardship is the answer here. Our lighting is comparatively good with ten parcan lights (a type of stage lighting). The challenge for us is to work toward more moving and percussive light and to learn the skills to use these worshipfully and well. We have not done much with dance except with liturgical dancers "up front" on occasion. Our congregation does move with the music and can do much more with dance carefully planned, prepared, and initially done within their "comfort zone." Other steps include the development of dance, drama, and light teams.

We are building a sound children and youth program with Dorothy Saunders-Perez, who is fluent in both English and Spanish. A next step is to build a computer lab where our young people can learn or improve these technical skills and help prepare materials for worship. We already have the gift of four adequate computers to begin.

Our worship is built around the church year, and Scripture is a central part of the worship. Next moves for us are more multisensory and multimedia presentations of the biblical text. Our worship is based in classical patterns of liturgy, and we need only to move to a more immersive service. A number of places in the worship can be very appropriately danced. I see especially the receiving of the elements in the Eucharist as one of these times, something that the St. Gregory of Nyssa Episcopal Church does very well in San Francisco.

The exciting part of all of this is putting it together in worship: the cohesive development of a service where figural ensemble serves the liturgy, where image, music, beat, light, move, and dance engage a performing congregation in an immersive environment of God's story. Worship and witness of this kind opens a host of ways to expand and to supplement the church's prophetic work. It is a context of embodied, immersive affirmation where the necessary work of prophetic criticism can also be done. It offers the opportunity for a church to be an alternative community of faith able to love the world but also able to oppose it and to call it into question.

Notes

1. Story and Practice

1. See, for example, *The Hauerwas Reader*, edited by John Berkman and Michael Cartwright (Durham: Duke University Press, 2001), Part II.

2. See John Webster, *Barth's Ethics of Reconciliation* (Cambridge: Cambridge University Press, 1995), 26. I am indebted to Stanley Hauerwas for calling this to my attention. See his *With the Grain of the Universe*, chapter 7, note 13.

3. I am indebted to Brad J. Kallenberg for calling my attention to Berkhof's analogy. See his *Live to Tell: Evangelism for a Postmodern Age* (Grand Rapids, Mich.: Brazos Press, 2002), 51.

4. See Dean Hoge, Benton Johnson, and Donald Luidens, *Vanishing Boundaries: The Religion of Mainline Protestant Baby Boomers* (Louisville: Westminster/John Knox, 1994), 184. The idea of "notions" is an old Quaker concept and is used by Dean Kelley, *Why Conservative Churches Are Growing* (New York: Harper & Row, 1972), 81.

5. I am indebted to my friends Bruce and Bonnie Williams for this story from their "Christmas Letter 1991."

2. Pitching Tent

1. See, for example, *The Hauerwas Reader*, edited by John Berkman and Michael Cartwright (Durham: Duke University Press, 2001), 228-29, 231-33, 248-49.

2. I am indebted here to Stanley Hauerwas, *The Hauerwas Reader*, 380, 391.

3. Hauerwas argues that the church does not have a culture, it is a culture. Hauerwas often makes this important claim. See, for example, *Sanctify Them in the Truth* (Nashville: Abingdon Press, 1998), 157-73.

4. See Stanley Hauerwas, *Christian Existence Today* (Durham, N.C.: Duke University Press, 1988), 121f.

5. *Theological Dictionary of the New Testament*, edited by Gerhard Kittel and Gerhard Friedrich and translated and abridged in one volume by Geoffrey W. Bromiley (Grand Rapids, Mich.: William B. Eerdmans Publishing Co., 1985), 1043.

6. *The Message: The New Testament, Psalms and Proverbs.* Copyright by Eugene H. Peterson, 1993, 1994, 1995, 1996, 1997, 1998, 1999, 2000, 2001, 2002, 2003. Used by permission of NavPress Publishing Group, John 1:14.

7. Kittel and Friedrich, *Theological Dictionary*, 1043.

8. John Milbank makes the important point that the idea of Incarnation must not take the place of the concrete narrative level of Jesus' life, teaching, death and resurrection. See *Theology and Social Theory* (Oxford: Basil Blackwell, 1990), 382-88, especially 384.

9. Terry Eagleton says that "to inhabit a language is already by that very token to inhabit a good deal more than it," and that that "which transcends language is exactly what the interior of our language informs us of." *The Illusions of Postmodernism* (Oxford: Blackwell Publishers, 1996), 13.

10. Susan VanZanten Gallagher, "Linguistic Power," *Christian Century* (March 12, 1997): 261.

11. See Werner H. Kelber, *The Oral and the Written Gospel* (Philadelphia: Fortress Press, 1983) for an explication of place of oral culture and its practices in Jesus' ministry and teaching, especially the Gospel of Mark.

12. Walter Wink, *Engaging the Powers* (Minneapolis: Fortress, 1992), p. 129, see 129-34.

13. Milbank is arguing in part here with George Lindbeck's position in *The Nature of Doctrine: Religion and Theology in a Postliberal Age* (London: S.P.C.K., 1984). Lindbeck attempts to abstract a set of a few simple rules—Christocentricity, for example, is one such "rule"—for interpreting the stories. Milbank judges that this fails to deal with the structural complexity of narratives and runs risks of rigidity and ahistoricity, 385.

14. Milbank, *Theology and Social Theory*, 385.

15. Ibid., 387.

16. Ibid.

17. Ibid., 386. I am substituting "pattern" and "story" for Milbank's language of *paradigmatic* and *syntagmatic*, which I find unnecessarily esoteric.

18. Ibid., 385.

19. John Milbank, *Word Made Strange: Theology, Language, Culture* (Williston, Vt.: Blackwell Publishers, 1997). See his wonderful and daunting chapter "Pleonasm, Speech and Writing," 55-83, especially 69-72 and 77-81. Milbank addresses here repetition and variation in relationship to speech and writing, but this notion of "non-identical repetition" can certainly be seen in relation to other practices.

20. Ibid., 32.

21. See, for example, Stanley Hauerwas and William H. Willimon, *Resident Aliens* (Nashville: Abingdon Press, 1989), 21.

22. See Michel Foucault, *Power-Knowledge: Selected Interviews and Other Writings, 1972–1977* (New York: Pantheon Books, 1980), 118-20 and 41-42. Foucault is clear here, however, that such constructions are not absolute, and resistance is possible within these.

23. William T. Cavanaugh, "Killing for the Telephone Company: Why the Nation State Is Not the Keeper of the Common Good," *Modern Theology*, 20.2 (April 2004): 243-74.

3. Multisensory, Multimedia Rhetoric

1. In an early work, the *Gryllos*, Aristotle's position is similar to Plato's in the *Gorgias*, but in the *Rhetoric* a quite different view emerges.

2. William C. Placher, *The Domestication of Transcendence: How Modern Thinking About God Went Wrong* (Louisville: Westminster John Knox Press, 1996), 54.

3. This is a quotation from William J. Bouwsma, *John Calvin: A Sixteenth-Century Portrait* (New York: Oxford University Press, 1988), 230-31. Quoted in Placher, 55.

4. Except when I am quoting Calvin, my use of the word *accommodate* is a negative one. I mean by it a certain kind of "selling out" of the faith. Calvin means something quite different.

5. *Commentaries on the Prophet Ezekiel* (on Ezek. 9:3-4), vol. 1, trans. Thomas Myers, *Calvin's Commentaries* 11:304. Quoted in Placher, 55-56.

6. Calvin, *Sermon 34 on Job* (on Job 9:7-15), *Opera,* vol. 33 (Brunsvigae: C. A. Schwetschke et filium, 1887), col. 423. Quoted in Placher, 57.

7. Calvin, *Commentaries on the Four Last Books of Moses* (on Exod. 33:20), vol. 3, trans. Charles William Bingham, *Calvin's Commentaries*, 3:381. Quoted in Placher, 58.

8. Calvin, Sermon 42 (on Deut. 5:22), *Sermons on Deuteronomy*, trans. Arthur Golding (Edinburgh: Banner of Truth Trust, 1987), 249, spelling modernized. Quoted in Placher, 58.

9. Placher, 58.

10. Manuel Castells, *The Rise of the Network Society: The Information Age: Economy, Society and Culture*, Vol. I (Oxford: Blackwell Publishers, 1996), 328.

11. Ibid., 373.

12. For perhaps the clearest example of such a critic by a philosopher of some renown, see Jean Baudrillard, *Simulacra and Simulation*, trans. Sheila Faria Glaser (Ann Arbor, Mich.: University of Michigan Press, 1999).

13. Sut Jhally, "Image-Based Culture: Advertising and Popular Culture," in Gail Dines and Jean M. Humez, eds., *Gender, Race and Class in Media* (Thousand Oaks, Calif.: Sage Publications, 1995), 83.

14. Stuart Ewen, *All Consuming Images: The Politics of Style in Contemporary Culture* (New York: Basic Books, 1988), 271. Quoted in Jhally, 85.

15. Jhally, "Image-Based Culture," 85.

16. Ibid., 86.

17. This comment by Jhally, however, does not take into account the increasing use of video cameras and recording devices by a growing number of people across the society. It may be that this is changing and rapidly. I will offer below a suggestion for the church to engage more deeply in the production of multimedia work, which can counter Jhally's critique.

18. Ibid.

19. Chris Jenks, ed., "The Centrality of the Eye in Western Culture," *Visual Culture* (London: Routledge, 1995), 10-14. The concept is one used by Martin Jay and taken up by Jenks. See Jay, "Scopic Regimes of Modernity," in Scott Lash and J. Friedman (eds.) *Modernity and Identity* (Oxford: Blackwell Publishers, 1992).

20. Jenks, *Visual Culture*, 3.

21. Saussure at the beginning of the last century, ordinary language philosophy, the work of Wittgenstein especially, the coming of linguistic studies on a major scale, and the more recent work of Lacan, Kristeva, Foucault, Lyotard, and Derrida among others are major contributors to this development.

22. Brad Kallenberg's *Ethics as Grammar* (Notre Dame: Notre Dame University Press, 2001) does a fine job of laying out Wittgenstein's mature position on his use of the concept "form of life," and on the complex relations between language and world. See chapter 5, esp. 190-92.

4. Imagophobia and the Use of Images

1. Nelson Goodman, *Languages and Art: An Approach to a Theory of Symbols*, 2d ed. (Indianapolis: Hackett Publishing, 1976), 247-48. Italics his. I am indebted to David Freedberg, *The Power of Images* (Chicago: The University of Chicago Press, 1989), 25, for pointing out this comment, but do not miss the further elaboration of Goodman, 248-52.

2. Ibid.

3. Freedberg, *Power of Images*, 430.

4. Ibid.

5. Ibid., 430-31.

6. Ibid., 378.

7. Ibid., 384.

8. William Dyrness, *Visual Faith: Art, Theology, and Worship in Dialogue* (Grand Rapids, Mich.: Baker Academic, 2001), 83.

9. Ibid.

10. I am indebted to Robert Barron for pointing out this distinction. See "Considering the Systematic Theology of James William

McClendon, Jr.," *Modern Theology*, 18.2 (April 2002): 272. But see for a fuller statement Jean-Luc Marion, *God Without Being* (Chicago: University of Chicago Press, 1991), 7-24.

11. Ibid.

12. Freedberg, *Power of Images*, 374.

13. I appreciate in this connection the fine work of Frank Burch Brown which addresses a number of these questions in terms of aesthetics in religious life. See his *Good Taste, Bad Taste, and Christian Taste* (New York: Oxford University Press, 2000).

14. Goodman, *Languages of Art*, 262. Quoted in Freedberg, *Power of Images*, 433.

15. Ibid.

16. Ibid., 356.

17. Ibid., 358.

18. W. J. T. Mitchell, *Iconology: Image, Text, Ideology* (Chicago: University of Chicago Press, 1987), 110. Quoted in Freedberg, *Power of Images*, 375.

19. Marius von Senden, *Space and Sight* (New York: The Free Press, 1960), quoted in S. Morris Engel, *The Study of Philosophy*, 2nd ed. (San Diego: Collegiate Press, 1987), 265-67. I do a fuller report of this research in *The Spectacle of Worship in a Wired World* (Nashville: Abingdon Press, 1998), 25-26.

20. Susanne Langer, *Philosophy in a New Key* (Cambridge, Mass.: Harvard University Press, 1941), 96-97.

21. Quoted in Collin Fry, "The Art of Seeing," *American Artist* (April 2002): 50.

22. Paul Messaris, *Visual "Literacy": Image, Mind, and Reality* (San Francisco: Westview Press, 1994), 118.

23. Messaris, *Visual "Literacy,"* 40. Messaris takes a position in which he seems to describe images "for what they are." He seems to hold to a view that we can distinguish what is really real and what is mediated. I find this view of the "real" and his view of the mediated to be inadequately developed. So far as I can tell, our understandings of the "real" are mediated. See ibid., 39-40, 70, and 176.

24. Ibid., 115.

25. Ibid.

26. W. J. T. Mitchell maintains that "there is no essential difference between poetry and painting, that is, that is given for all time by the inherent natures of the media, the objects they represent, or the laws of the human mind." Yet, cultures do make distinctions: "There are always a number of differences in effect in a culture which allow it to sort out the distinctive qualities of its ensemble of signs and symbols." His work raises the question of whether any line can finally be drawn between image and word that applies across history and culture. See his *Image, Text, Ideology* (Chicago: University of Chicago Press, 1986), 49.

27. Hauerwas's view of story is key here. See his important essay, "God's New Language" in *The Hauerwas Reader*, 142-62, especially 155.

28. Langer, *Philosophy in a New Key*, 145.

29. Gerard Loughlin, *Telling God's Story* (Cambridge: University of Cambridge Press, 1999), 23.

30. Mitchell Stephens, *The Rise of the Image The Fall of the Word* (Oxford: Oxford University Press, 1998), 201.

31. Ibid., 151-89.

32. Walter Benjamin, *Illuminations* (New York: Schocken Books, 1968), 234. Quoted in Stephens, 111.

5. Sound as Music and Beat

1. Ruth Finnegan, *The Hidden Musicians* (Cambridge: Cambridge University, 1989), passim. Simon Frith notes two problems with Finnegan's research. First, because the town she studies is a white town, she is not "able to say much about music and ethnicity." Second, she is not able to pay enough attention "to the media and what one might call genre's fantasy communities . . .," with media's various impact from genre to genre, its effect on musicians, and its different effect on consumers. See *Performing Rites* (Cambridge: Harvard University Press, 1996), 299, n.35, n. 36.

2. This is a phrase of Martin Luther King Jr. that he used many times in his speeches and sermons.

3. Kris Kristofferson, "Help Me Make It Through the Night."

4. Susanne Langer, *Feeling and Form* (New York: Charles Scribner's Sons, 1953), 27.

5. Ibid., 32.

6. Simon Frith, *Performing Rites: On the Value of Popular Music* (Cambridge: Harvard University Press, 1996), 272.

7. Ibid.

8. Ibid. Italics in the original. See John Miller Chernoff, *African Rhythm and African Sensibility* (Chicago: University of Chicago Press, 1979), 36.

9. See Edward Lippman, *A History of Western Musical Aesthetics* (Lincoln: University of Nebraska Press, 1992). See especially chapter 12, "Theories of Meaning."

10. Quoted by Pinchas Noy, "The Psychodynamic of Music, Part 1," *Journal of Music Therapy* 3 (4) 1966: 127.

11. See my discussion of this difference in *The Spectacle of Worship in a Wired World*, 81-83.

12. James Edwards does a nice job with this distinction in Wittgenstein's work. See *Ethics Without Philosophy* (Tampa: The University Presses of Florida, 1982), 195-98.

13. Roger Scruton, a British scholar who works with analytic philosophy, argues that our ability in language for metaphoric transfer is basic to our understanding of music. "If we take away the metaphors of movement, of space, of chords as objects, of melodies as advancing and retreating, as moving up and down—if we take those metaphors away, nothing of music remains, but only sound." "Understanding Music," in his *The Aesthetic Understanding: Essays in the Philosophy of Art and Culture*, 85. Quoted in Lippman, *A History of Western Musical Aesthetics*, 390. Simon Frith maintains that music is "an adjectival experience." The use of adjectives is "a necessary aspect of all music listening." Frith, *Performing Rites*, 263, 264.

14. Brian Wren, *Praying Twice* (Louisville: Westminster/John Knox, 2000), 127-66.

15. Libretto by Giuseppe Giacosa and Luigi Illica, based on episodes from Henri Murger's, copyright G. Ricordi & Company.

16. Frith, *Performing Rites*, 178-80.

17. See Ludwig Wittgenstein, *Zettel*. Edited by G. E. M. Anscombe and G. H. von Wright. Translated by G. E. M. Anscombe (Berkeley:

University of California Press, 1970), section 32 and *On Certainty*, section 56. I am indebted to Brad J. Kallenberg for pointing this out to me. See his *Ethics as Grammar* (Notre Dame: University of Notre Dame Press, 2001), 108.

18. See my *The Spectacle of Worship in a Wired World*, 34-44.

19. See Susan McClary, "Same As It Ever Was," *Microphone Fiends*. Edited by Andrew Ross and Tricia Rose (London: Routledge, 1994), 35-36. See also her *Feminine Endings* (Minneapolis: University of Minnesota Press, 1991), 23-24.

20. Dom Moio does a fine job of both displaying the rhythms of these genres on a score, and then of playing them on a CD. See his *Latin Percussion in Perspective* (Pacific, Mo.: Mel Bay Publications, 1997).

6. Let There Be Light

1. Arthur Zajonc, *Catching the Light: The Entwined History of Light and Mind* (Oxford: Oxford University Press, 1993).

2. Richard Pilbrow, *Stage Lighting Design: The Art, The Craft, The Life* (New York: Design Press, 2000), 3. Pilbrow's book is expecially good on the technical aspects of stage lighting. For an extended treatment of the aesthetics of stage lighting see Richard H. Palmer, *The Lighting Art: The Aesthetics of Lighting Design*, 2d edition (Englewood Cliffs, N.J.: Prentice Hall, 1994). Palmer's work is the best book I know on the aesthetics of lighting design and is a treasure in this regard. Also very helpful are Drew Campbell, *Technical Theater for Nontechnical People* (New York: Allworth Press, 1999), and Graham Walters, *Stage Lighting Step-By-Step: The Complete Guide on Setting the Stage with Light to Get Dramatic Results* (Cincinnati: Betterway Books, 1997).

3. Pilbrow, *Stage Lighting Design*, 4.

4. Ibid., 4.

5. Ibid.

6. Palmer, *The Lighting Art,* 13.

7. Pilbrow, 5.

8. Ibid., 5.

9. Ibid., 5.
10. Ibid.
11. Ibid.
12. Ibid., 6.
13. Ibid.
14. Ibid., 7.
15. Ibid., 8.
16. Ibid., 9.

7. Movement and Dance

1. "Acts of John, the Hymn of Christ." Quoted in Jürgen Moltmann, *The Spirit of Life: A Universal Affirmation* (Minneapolis: Fortress Press, 1992), 19.

2. M.G.M. musical film. Music and lyrics by Arthur Freed and Nacio Herb Brown, 1952.

3. Langer, *Feeling and Form*, 49.

4. Ibid.

5. Ibid., 50.

6. Ibid., 24.

7. Let me register but qualify my appreciation for Langer's work. I find myself in disagreement with her epistemological method and her metaphysics. I also have trouble with the way she characterizes "the masses." Yet, when one works with her thought as descriptions of uses of art, her work is extraordinarily helpful.

8. I appreciate Gene Lowry's contribution in helping me think through this issue, though he does not agree with where I come out.

9. Langer, *Feeling and Form*, 174.

10. Ibid., 175.

11. Ibid.

12. Ibid.

13. Francis Sparshott, *Off the Ground: First Steps to a Philosophical Consideration of the Dance* (Princeton, N.J.: Princeton University Press, 1988), 206. Quoted in Frith, *Performing Rites*, 220.

14. Frith, *Performing Rites*, 220.

15. Quoted in Judith Lynne Hanna, "Dance," *Ethnomusicology:*

An Introduction. Edited by Helen Myers (New York: W. W. Norton, 1992), 323.

16. Ibid., 324.

17. Ibid., 322-23.

8. Figural Ensemble in Performance, Story, and Immersion

1. Walter Ong, *The Presence of the Word* (Minneapolis: The University of Minnesota Press, 1967), 115.

2. Ibid., 117.

3. See "Women in Rock" (New York: Time Warner Company, 1986).

4. Langer, *Feeling and Form*, 184.

5. *Webster's New Universal Dictionary of the English Language* (New York: Webster's International Press, 1976).

6. See Sherry Turkle, *Life on the Screen* (New York: Simon & Schuster, Touchstone Books, 1995). Turkle writes of two aesthetics arising from the use of computer: one that of the "culture of calculation" and the other that of the "culture of simulation." The former is the modern approach, the latter is postmodern. The first focuses on analysis and searches for depth and mechanism. The latter is a process of inhabitation and exploration. Her work here names some of the sources of the change from print modes of distancing to those of immersion due to the coming of the computer with its capacity for simulation. My focus on immersion comes more from popular culture, especially from concerts and public venues of that kind. An interesting study could come from the examination of these two and their mutually influencing each other. See also Scott Lash, *The Sociology of Postmodernity* (London: Routledge, 1990). He discusses modernity as operating through a distancing of the spectator from the cultural object in contrast to a postmodern immersion of the spectator, 175ff.

7. B. Joseph Pine II and James H. Gilmore, "Welcome to the Experience Economy," *Harvard Business Review* (July-August 1998): 97-

105. They subsequently published their book, *The Experience Economy* (Cambridge: Harvard University Press, 1999).

8. Ibid., 102.

9. Ibid., 102-4.

9. The Prophetic Use of Figure in Hebrew Poetry

1. John Milbank, *The Word Made Strange: Theology, Language, Culture* (Oxford: Blackwell Publishers, 1997), 55-83. Milbank engages here the work of Warburton, Lowth, Vico, and Hamann and examines their arguments about the origin of language. His concern is a use of language and culture that does not simply advance established power in a society. He is responding directly to Nietzsche, Foucault, and Derrida. Basic to his point is that if language and culture are really only instruments of power and coercion, then any theological language is an extrinsic means to serve the interests of power. Milbank sees this kind of claim as a transcendental one that cannot be made philosophically since there are no foundations in reason or experience that can sustain such arguments. Could such arguments be made, they would, of course, undermine the work of theology and the faith claims of the church.

2. Milbank, *Word Made Strange*, 65.

3. Ibid.

4. Ibid., 66. Italics are Milbank's.

5. Ibid., 69.

6. Ibid., 66.

7. Ibid., 69.

8. Ibid., 70.

9. Ibid.

10. Milbank is arguing with Derrida here. He says: "If the sign is not oral, if it is not also an embodied event with a certain concrete 'expression' of what it conveys, if it is not also something which dies, can be wiped out, forgotten, but is *defined* (as Derrida explicitly defines it) by its survival of the death of the speaker, or of any empirical existence, then, as Catherine Pickstock argues, it *is* death, *is* 'the impossible,' *is* absolute deferral, *is* no-thing: the ideal. The absolute

stasis, formalism, obscurity and fetishized capacity for *manipulative tyranny* of the regime of 'pure writing' (as identified by Socrates in *Phaedrus*) is *preserved* by Derrida, and simply more precisely defined—as nihilism." Quoted in Milbank, 70-71.

11. "Such a notion of repetition is an inherently 'oral' one, since it relates it . . . to the vast *number* of synonymous signs in spoken inflection available, thereby allying words in their 'copiousness' *as far as possible* (and new words can be minted, just as words can die) to the variety and change of life itself, to history, and the 'spoken' performance of sign which is necessary for there to be a sign at all" (71, italics his). On the repetitious and copious character of oral culture, see Walter Ong, *Orality and Literacy* (London: Routledge, 1982), 39-40.

10. The Prophetic Use of Figure in Electronic Culture

1. Emphasis mine. See *Orality and Literacy*, 136, and 135-38. Cf. Ong's *The Presence of the Word* (Minneapolis: University of Minneapolis Press, 1967), 87-92. While Ong's work here is from the 1960s and largely from a "television world," nevertheless I continue to find his work quite stimulating and helpful.

2. Scott Lash, *The Sociology of Postmodernism* (London: Routledge, 1990), 194.

3. See his book by that title, *The Rise of the Image The Fall of the Word* (New York: Oxford University Press, 1998).

4. Lash, 194.

5. I recently did a paper in which I distinguish the practices of significance from those of the practices of importance. I suggest there that the church in its worship is not versed in the practices of impact, though it continues to work with the practices of most importance like worship, prayer, Eucharist, and ministries of service and justice. I suggest there new directions to address this problem. See "The Practices of Significance," *The Living Pulpit*, 12.3 (July/September 2003): 36-37.

6. I am indebted to my friend, Bascom D. Talley III, for this example of *The Simpsons*.

7. Frank Rich, "Journal," *New York Times* (July 21, 1994), A-15.

8. Ibid.

9. Ibid.

10. Spencer Ebbinga, "Starting Over," *Video Portfolio* (Jan. 2001), unpublished.

11. Critical Immersion

1. Lawrence Grossberg, *Dancing in Spite of Myself* (Durham: Duke University Press, 1997), 111. James McClendon draws a distinction between convictions and opinions. To change one's convictions is to change notions so vital to us that to change them is to change ourselves, whereas a change in opinions requires no such shift. McClendon, *Doctrine: Systematic Theology,* Vol. 2 (Nashville: Abingdon Press, 1994), 29.

2. In the section above I draw from an article of mine, "The Practices of Significance," *The Living Pulpit* (July-September 2003): 36-37.

3. Frederic Jameson, *Postmodernism or The Cultural Logic of Late Capitalism* (Durham: Duke University Press, 1991), 48-49.

4. Eric Elnes is pastor of the Scottsdale Congregational United Church of Christ in Scottsdale, Arizona. It is a church of less than 300 members but does the most creative worship of a multisensory and multimedia form that I know. Elnes also holds a Ph.D. in Hebrew Scripture. He does not use the lectionary because of weaknesses he sees in it, but uses other means to be addressed by the full range of the biblical text.

5. I heard Leonard Sweet say this in a workshop, but see, for example, his *FAITHQUAKES* (Nashville: Abingdon Press, 1994), 46-50. For his more recent view of the centrality of experience, see Sweet, Brian D. McLaren, and Jerry Haselmayer, *A Is for Abductive* (Grand Rapids, Mich.: Zondervan, 2003), 119-23.

6. Michel de Certeau, *The Practices of Everyday Life* (Berkeley: University of California Press, 1984), xix, 36-39.

7. From the album "Stripped," 1995.

8. See Ludwig Wittgenstein, *On Certainty* (Oxford: Basil Blackwell, 1969), sec. 501. See the fine discussion of Wittgenstein's

use of objects of comparison in James Edwards, *Ethics without Philosophy*, 130, 143, 146, 173, 195, 200.

9. One can argue that each of the forms of critique above makes use of juxtaposition. I certainly have no need to deny it. But I do not want to reduce any one of the forms of critique to that of juxtaposition. For example, putting the world's story in God's story can be construed as a juxtaposition, but it strikes me as an important form of critique in its own terms. Something is lost in collapsing the two together.

10. These forms of critique occur in a good deal of Foucault's work. I am indebted here to a good sum of them by Steven Best and Douglas Kellner, *Postmodern Theory* (New York: The Guilford Press, 1991), 34-75.

Epilogue

1. I am indebted here to Charles Fulton of the Episcopal Church Building Fund for this idea of worship "in the round" with the use of two screens. I have learned a great deal from his background in church architecture.

Selected Bibliography

Barron, Robert. "Considering the Systematic Theology of James William McClendon, Jr." *Modern Theology* 18.2 (April 2002).

Baudrillard, Jean. *Simulacra and Simulation*. trans. Sheila Faria Glaser. Ann Arbor, Mich.: University of Michigan Press, 1999.

Benjamin, Walter. *Illuminations*. New York: Schocken Books, 1968.

Best, Steven, and Douglas Kellner. *Postmodern Theory*. New York: Guilford Press, 1991.

Bouwsma, William J. *John Calvin: A Sixteenth-Century Portrait*. New York: Oxford University Press, 1988.

Brown, Frank Burch. *Good Taste, Bad Taste, and Christian Taste*. New York: Oxford University Press, 2000.

Castells, Manuel. *The Rise of the Network Society: The Information Age: Economy, Society and Culture*, Vol. I. Oxford: Blackwell Publishers, 1996.

Certeau, Michel de. *The Practices of Everyday Life*. Berkeley: The University of California Press, 1984.

Chernoff, John Miller. *African Rhythm and African Sensibility*. Chicago: University of Chicago Press, 1979.

Dyrness, William. *Visual Faith: Art, Theology, and Worship in Dialogue*. Grand Rapids: Baker Academic, 2001.

Eagleton, Terry. *The Illusions of Postmodernism*. Oxford: Blackwell Publishers, 1996.

Edwards, James. *Ethics Without Philosophy*. Tampa: The University Presses of Florida, 1982.

Engel, S. Morris. *The Study of Philosophy*. 2nd ed. San Diego: Collegiate Press, 1987.

Ewen, Stuart. *All Consuming Images: The Politics of Style in Contemporary Culture*. New York: Basic Books, 1988.

Finnegan, Ruth. *The Hidden Musicians*. Cambridge: Cambridge University Press, 1989.

Foucault, Michel. *Power-Knowledge: Selected Interviews and Other Writings, 1972–1977*. New York: Pantheon Books, 1980.

Freedberg, David. *The Power of Images: Studies in the History and Theory of Response*. Chicago: The University of Chicago Press, 1989.

Frith, Simon. *Performing Rites: On the Value of Popular Music*. Cambridge: Harvard University Press, 1996.

Fry, Collin. "The Art of Seeing," *American Artist* (April 2002), 50.

Gallagher, Susan VanZanten. "Linguistic Power," *Christian Century* (March 12, 1997).

Goodman, Nelson. *Languages and Art: An Approach to a Theory of Symbols*. 2d ed. Indianapolis: Hackett Publishing, 1976.

Grossberg, Lawrence. *Dancing in Spite of Myself*. Durham: Duke University Press, 1997.

Hanna, Judith Lynne. "Dance," in Helen Myers (ed.), *Ethnomusicology: An Introduction*. New York: W. W. Norton, 1992.

Hauerwas, Stanley. *Christian Existence Today*. Durham: Duke University Press, 1988.

———. *Sanctify Them in the Truth*. Nashville: Abingdon Press, 1998.

———. *The Hauerwas Reader*, edited by John Berkman and Michael Cartwright. Durham: Duke University Press, 2001.

———. *With the Grain of the Universe: The Gifford Lectures of 2001*. Grand Rapids, Mich.: Brazos Press, 2001.

———. and William H. Willimon. *Resident Aliens*. Nashville: Abingdon Press, 1989.

Hoge, Dean, Benton Johnson, and Donald Luidens. *Vanishing Boundaries: The Religion of Mainline Protestant Baby Boomers*. Louisville: Westminster/John Knox, 1994.

Jameson, Frederic. *Postmodernism or The Cultural Logic of Late Capitalism*. Durham: Duke University Press, 1991.

Jay, Martin. "Scopic Regimes of Modernity" in Scott Lash and J. Friedman (eds.), *Modernity and Identity*. Oxford: Blackwell Publishers, 1992.

Jenks, Chris, ed. "The Centrality of the Eye in Western Culture," in *Visual Culture.* London: Routledge, 1995.

Jhally, Sut. "Image-Based Culture: Advertising and Popular Culture," in Gail Dines and Jean M. Humez (eds.), *Gender, Race and Class in Media.* Thousand Oaks, Cal.: Sage Publications, 1995.

Kallenberg, Brad. *Ethics as Grammar.* Notre Dame: Notre Dame University Press, 2001.

———. *Live to Tell: Evangelism for a Postmodern Age.* Grand Rapids, Mich.: Brazos Press, 2002.

Kelber, Werner H. *The Oral and the Written Gospel.* Philadelphia: Fortress Press, 1983.

Kelley, Dean M. *Why Conservative Churches Are Growing: A Study in Sociology of Religion.* New York: Harper & Row, 1972.

Kittel Gerhard, and Gerhard Friedrich, eds. *Theological Dictionary of the New Testament.* Translated and abridged in one volume by Geoffrey W. Bromiley. Grand Rapids, Mich.: William B. Eerdmans, 1985.

Langer, Susanne. *Feeling and Form.* New York: Charles Scribner's Sons, 1953.

———. *Philosophy in a New Key.* Cambridge, Mass.: Harvard University Press, 1941.

Lash, Scott. *The Sociology of Postmodernity.* London: Routledge, 1990.

Lindbeck, George. *The Nature of Doctrine: Religion and Theology in a Postliberal Age.* London: S.P.C.K., 1984.

Lippman, Edward. *A History of Western Musical Aesthetics.* Lincoln: University of Nebraska Press, 1992.

Loughlin, Gerard. *Telling God's Story.* Cambridge: University of Cambridge Press, 1999.

McClary. Susan. *Feminine Endings.* Minneapolis: University of Minnesota Press, 1991.

———. "Same As It Ever Was," in *Microphone Fiends.* Edited by Andrew Ross and Tricia Rose. London: Routledge, 1994.

Messaris, Paul. *Visual "Literacy": Image, Mind, and Reality.* San Francisco: Westview Press, 1994.

Selected Bibliography

Milbank, John. *Theology and Social Theory: Beyond Secular Reason*. Oxford: Basil Blackwell, 1990.

———. *The Word Made Strange: Theology, Language, Culture*. Oxford: Blackwell Publishers, 1997.

Mitchell, W. J. T., *Iconology: Image, Text, Ideology*. Chicago: University of Chicago Press, 1987.

Moio, Dom, *Latin Percussion in Perspective*. Pacific, Mo.: Mel Bay Publications, 1997.

Myers, Helen, ed. *Ethnomusicology: An Introduction*. New York: W. W. Norton, 1992.

Ong, Walter, *Orality and Literacy*. London: Routledge, 1982.

———. *The Presence of the Word*. Minneapolis: University of Minnesota Press, 1967.

Palmer, Richard H. *The Lighting Art: The Aesthetics of Lighting Design*. 2d ed. Englewood Cliffs, N.J.: Prentice Hall, 1994.

Peterson, Eugene H. *The Message: The New Testament, Psalms and Proverbs*. Copyright by Eugene H. Peterson, 1993, 1994, 1995, 1996, 1997, 1998, 1999, 2000, 2001, 2002, 2003. Used by permission of NavPress Publishing Group.

Pickstock, Catherine. *After Writing: On the Liturgical Consummation of Philosophy*. Oxford: Blackwell Publishers, Inc., 1998.

Pilbrow, Richard. *Stage Lighting Design: The Art, The Craft, The Life*. New York: Design Press, 2000.

Pine II, B. Joseph, and James H. Gilmore. *The Experience Economy*. Cambridge: Harvard University Press, 1999.

———. "Welcome to the Experience Economy," *Harvard Business Review* (July-August, 1998).

Placher, William C. *The Domestication of Transcendence: How Modern Thinking About God Went Wrong*. Louisville: Westminster John Knox Press, 1996.

Puccini, Giacomo. *La Bohème*. Libretto by Giuseppe Giacosa and Luigi Illica, based on episodes from Henri Murger's *Scenes de la vie de Bohème*. G. Ricordi & Company, 1896.

Rich, Frank. "Journal," *New York Times* (July 21, 1994), A-15.

202

Sample, Tex. *The Spectacle of Worship in a Wired World.* Nashville: Abingdon Press, 1998.

———. "The Practices of Significance," *The Living Pulpit*, 12.3 (July/September 2003).

Scruton, Roger. *The Aesthetic Understanding: Essays in the Philosophy of Art and Culture.* London: St. Augustine's Press, 1983.

Sparshott, Francis. *Off the Ground: First Steps to a Philosophical Consideration of the Dance.* Princeton, N.J.: Princeton University Press, 1988.

Stephens, Mitchell. *The Rise of the Image The Fall of the Word.* Oxford: Oxford University Press, 1998.

Sweet, Leonard. *FAITHQUAKES.* Nashville: Abingdon Press, 1994.

———. Brian D. McLaren, and Jerry Haselmayer. *A Is For Abductive.* Grand Rapids: Zondervan, 2003.

Turkle, Sherry. *Life on the Screen.* New York: Simon & Schuster, Touchstone Books, 1995.

von Senden. Marius. *Space and Sight.* New York: The Free Press, 1960.

Webster, John. *Barth's Ethics of Reconciliation.* Cambridge: Cambridge University Press, 1995.

Wink, Walter. *Engaging the Powers.* Minneapolis: Fortress, 1992.

Wittgenstein, Ludwig. *On Certainty.* Edited by G. E. M. Anscombe and G. H. von Wright. Translated by Denis Paul and G. E. M. Anscombe. New York: Harper & Row, 1969.

———. *Philosophical Investigations.* Translated by G. E. M. Anscombe. Oxford: Basil Blackwell, 1953.

———. *Zettel.* Edited by G. E. M. Anscombe and G. H. von Wright. Translated by G. E. M. Anscombe. Berkeley: University of California Press, 1970.

Wren, Brian. *Praying Twice.* Louisville: Westminster/John Knox, 2000.

Zajonc, Arthur. *Catching the Light: The Entwined History of Light and Mind.* Oxford: Oxford University Press, 1993.

Index

205

Index

206

Index

Index